Accounting for IT Professionals

A guide to basic components of an accounting database

Chris Chinaire

To my son, Ruvheneko, whose first impression of accounting inspired the book. And my wife and friend, Tembi, for unwavering support in every season.

Table of Contents

About the Author

Chris Chinaire is a certified data management and business intelligence professional (CDMP, CBIP) with a solid grasp of financial and accounting systems.

He has over 28 years industry experience during which he played key roles in architecting, building and customising financial information solutions for corporations in finance, legal and medical sectors.

Preface

The modern information technology (IT) professional is expected to have multiple cross-functional competencies. The days of one-dimensional technocrats have come and gone. An IT professional is expected to be a master of all trades and a jack of none.

The demands are no different to those placed on a professional football (soccer) player who is presumed to be fit, good with both feet, solid in the air, a strong tackler, good passer, goal scorer, and reader of the game.

Accounting, the language of business, is one of key competencies expected in an IT professional. Unfortunately, many have an accounting phobia instilled by a combination of mental Ctrl+Alt+Del reflex actions to accounting jargon and perceived complexity of accounting software. To be fair, some legacy accounting systems are not logically structured, though accounting itself is logical and structured.

This book was written by an IT professional to present a view of the mechanics of accounting through a database lens. A simple data model is used to illustrate application of concepts in processing transactions and creating accounting data. Predetermined logic ordinarily held in the minds of accounting practitioners is stored in database tables, enabling automation of repeatable processes and eliminating the need to memorise basics.

Examples of TSQL code are included to illustrate data retrieval for preparation of standard reports. TSQL (Transact-SQL) is Microsoft's and Sybase's proprietary extension to the SQL used to interact with relational databases.

This is not a gateway to a career change neither is it a blueprint of the mother of all accounting systems—intricacies are omitted to magnify core concepts. The primary goal is to debunk the notion that accounting is complex and hopefully redress IT's underrepresentation in the middle ground shared with accounting.

Chapter 1: Introduction

What is accounting?

Accounting is a data management system that transforms financial transactions into meaningful information for decision making. Raw data in the form of financial transactions is recorded, classified, and summarised into structured data stores from which financial information is prepared as depicted in the flowchart below.

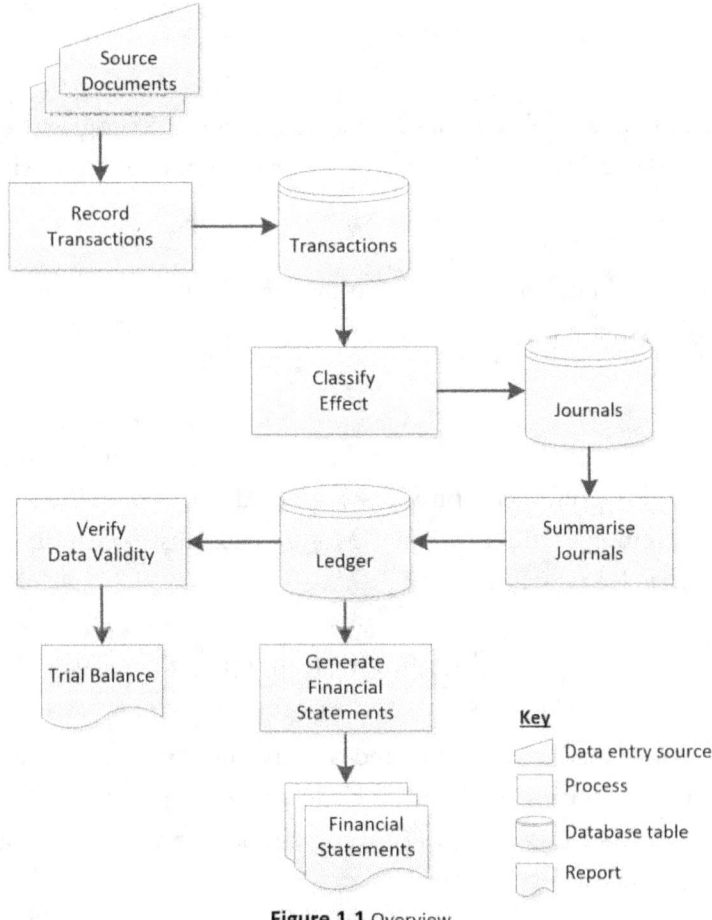

Figure 1.1 Overview

Effects of transactions are recorded in chronological order in the journal data store and summarised by month in the ledger, from which financial information is retrieved as financial statements

Usage of financial information

Managers use financial information to monitor performance and take measures required to improve results. Owners use the same information to assess the viability of their investment and decide course of action. Employees' focus is job security and timing of pay-raise negotiations.

Suppliers' primary concern is the creditworthiness of the business and its ability to pay for goods and services. Lenders use the information to gain an insight into the capability of the business to pay back loans. Tax authorities want to ensure the business is correctly taxed.

Legal structure

Examples in this book are based on a sole trader, the simplest legal structure for a business. A sole trader, also known as sole proprietorship, is a business owned and run by one person.

There is no legal distinction between the owner and the business. For accounting purposes business transactions are accounted for separately from the owner's personal transactions.

A fictitious sole trader, D Kay, trading as Dee Kay Distributors, is the basis of illustrations in this book. The business buys and sells computer consumables and stationery and employs three people. Monthly expenses include premises rental, salaries, gas, and electricity.

Types of processes

Three types of processes are covered—transaction, month end, and year end. The transaction process relates to the immediate processing of financial transactions as they occur. It covers fourteen types of transactions that include buying and selling of goods, paying expenses, and so on.

The month-end process involves checking the validity of data processed in a month, closing the financial month, producing financial reports, and opening the following month for transaction processing.

The year-end process, which happens after the month-end process of the last month of the year, encompasses closing the year, producing year-end financial reports, and opening the first month of the following year for transaction processing.

Database example

A database is used to process transactions and store accounting data. It is designed with the following goals in mind:

(a) Minimise ambiguity of application of accounting principles.
(b) Enable consistent processing of financial transactions.
(c) Support verification of data from summary to transactional detail.
(d) Facilitate efficient retrieval of data to produce financial statements.
(e) Allow retrospective production of financial statements.

Figure 1.2 shows the symbols used to portray the relationships between tables.

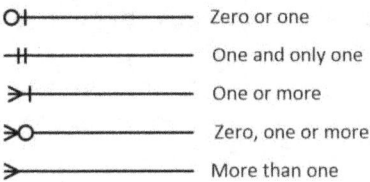

⊶	Zero or one
⊣⊢	One and only one
⋗⊢	One or more
⋗○	Zero, one or more
⋗	More than one

Figure 1.2 Relationship symbols

Anatomy of accounting data

Accounting data comes from transactions and is held in two forms—the journal and the ledger. The same data is expressed and stored in three different ways shown in Figure 1.3.

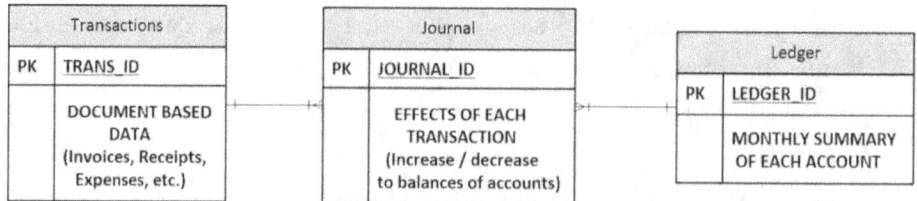

Figure 1.3 Anatomy of accounting data

The transactions data store contains document-based data. As the basis of accounting data, the records are referred to as source documents. The data is like a set of manual files containing copies of invoices, receipts, expenses, payments, and so on.

Most accounting systems have a transaction table for each type of transaction. For simplicity, one multipurpose table is used in examples in the book.

The journal is a chronicle of dual effects of transactions recorded as either increases or decreases to balances of accounts. It is the equivalent of a journal used in manual accounting systems. The data store is considered the book of original entry because it contains the first record of transactions in accounting format.

The ledger is an aggregate of journal data. It contains monthly summaries of effects of transactions and resultant balances of each account. Update of the ledger from journal summaries is called posting. Verified ledger data is the primary source of financial statements.

Chapter 2: Accounting Basics

Accounting equation

Accounting is based on the principle that resources owned by a business are equal to the resources that financed them.

A business is financed from two possible sources: the owner and loans. Resources owned by a business are called assets and resources supplied by the owner are referred to as equity. Liabilities are resources borrowed. This can be illustrated by the following relationship known as the accounting equation:

$$assets = liabilities + equity$$

The equation reflects how much of assets are financed by the owner and how much are owed to others. An increase in either liabilities or equity results in an equal increase in assets. Similarly, a decrease in either liabilities or equity is triggered by an equal decrease in assets.

Income generated, called revenue, increases assets and equity, while costs incurred, referred to as expenses, decrease assets and equity. Resources taken by the owner for personal use, called withdrawals, decrease assets and equity.

Effects of revenue, expenses, and withdrawals are applied to assets and liabilities immediately after a transaction occurs. But the impact to equity is deferred to the end of the financial year. So, during a financial year, reality is expressed by the expanded accounting equation:

$$assets = liabilities + equity + revenue - expenses - withdrawals$$

Revenue, expenses, and withdrawals are temporarily accumulated, and their overall effect is applied to equity at the end of each financial year, after which they are initialised to start the following year from zero.

The left side of the equation is called debit and the right side, credit. The algebra addition rule puts expenses and withdrawals on the debit side of the rewritten expression:

$$assets + expenses + withdrawals = liabilities + equity + revenue$$

The debit- and credit-side concept is extended to denote increase and decrease effects of each element triggered by transactions.

Elements on the debit side are increased by debits and decreased by credits, while credit-side elements are increased by credits and reduced by debits.

Table 2.1 shows that transaction 1 increases assets and equity, transaction 2 increases expenses and liabilities, and transaction 3 decreases assets and liabilities.

	Debit side						=	Credit side					
	Assets		Expenses		Withdrawal			Liabilities		Equity		Revenue	
	Debit	Credit	Debit	Credit	Debit	Credit		Debit	Credit	Debit	Credit	Debit	Credit
Transaction 1	X										X		
Transaction 2			X						X				
Transaction 3		X						X					

Table 2.1 Effect of transactions on elements of the accounting equation

The difference between debits and credits of each element results is either a debit or credit balance depending on the higher value. Debit-side elements are expected to have debit balances, whereas credit side elements are expected to have credit balances.

So, assets, expenses, and withdrawals have a normal debit balance, while liabilities, equity, and revenue have a normal credit balance. The overall debit balance is expected to be equal to the total credit balance.

The accounting equation is a recurring theme in accounting. It forms the foundation of the double-entry system, shapes database design, and guides tables' structure.

Transaction

A transaction is an exchange of resources involving two or more accounts and changes the financial position of a business. An increase or decrease of at least one element of the accounting equation constitutes a change in the financial position.

Only transactions that change the financial position of a business are recorded as accounting data.

Double entry

The double-entry principle is a recognition of the twofold aspect of every financial transaction. It is the systematic recording of two sides of an exchange.

A cash purchase of a laptop exchanges cash for a laptop. Double entry records the effect on cash on the one side and the impact on computer hardware on the other.

If the laptop is partly paid for in cash and the difference by cheque, then three accounts are involved in the resource exchange, including the bank account. The effects of the exchange, which are opposite and equal, are recorded as debits and credits.

Exchange of resources

Resources are exchanged in at least one of following four ways:

- Cash—for payments and receipts
- Bank—for payments and receipts through the bank
- Credit—for purchases and sales on credit
- Noncash asset—for resource contributions in physical assets (building, machinery, etc.), withdrawal of physical assets for own use by the owner, and so on.

Methods of exchange are held in the METHOD_OF_EXCHANGE table, listed in table 2.2.:

MOE_ID	EXCHANGE_METHOD
1	Cash
2	Bank
3	Credit
4	Non-cash asset

Table 2.2 Methods of exchange

Accounting methods

There are two methods of accounting—accrual and cash. The difference between the two is the timing of when revenue and expenses are recognized and recorded as accounting data.

The cash method accounts for revenue when money is received and for expenses when money is paid out. Updates to the journal and the ledger are, therefore, deferred until money is either received or paid out.

On the other hand, the accrual method accounts for revenue when it is earned and expenses when they are incurred, allowing for creation of journal entries and update of the ledger following transactions.

Most large businesses use the accrual method—the basis of examples in the book.

Perpetual and periodic inventory system

A perpetual inventory system keeps an up-to-date record of inventory held using a real-time point of sale system.

In contrast, a periodic inventory system requires a manual count at specific intervals to determine numbers and value of inventory sold and held.

Examples in the book are based on a perpetual inventory system.

Financial year and month

A financial year, also known as an accounting period, is the time frame of twelve consecutive months over which a business records, collates, and reports annual financial information.

The financial year does not always coincide with the calendar year. Similarly, a financial month may be based on either the calendar or specific date ranges, for example, March 15 to April 14, April 15 to May 14, and so on.

Financial years are held in the FINANCIAL_YEAR table and corresponding months in the FINANCIAL_MONTH table, as shown in Figure 2.1.

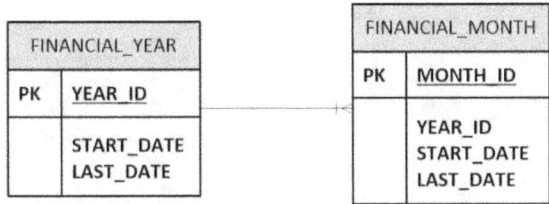

Figure 2.1 Financial periods

Periodic versus running balancing

The periodic method updates the ledger monthly. So, as part of the month-end process, journal entries are summarised and balances posted to the ledger.

On the other hand, the running-balance method keeps the ledger up-to-date by calculating and maintaining resultant balances of every journal entry.

Examples in this book use the running-balance method.

Chapter 3: Accounts

What is an account?

An account is the primary means of classification of effects of transactions. Accounts, therefore, enable tracking of business expenses and transactions with key stakeholders like the owner, the bank, lenders (creditors), suppliers of goods and services (creditors), tax authorities and customers (debtors).

Choice of accounts depends on the types of transactions anticipated and the level of detail required in reporting, creating a symbiotic relationship between accounts and transactions.

For one business, an office equipment account may be adequate, while reporting needs of another may be best served by separate accounts for photocopiers, servers, printers, desktops, and laptops.

Examples of accounts include office furniture, computer hardware, cash, bank account, rent, income, wages, electricity, and gas.

Accounts are logically grouped to facilitate both internal and external reporting.

Categories

Categories are the top-level grouping of accounts and represent the six elements of the expanded accounting equation: assets, liabilities, equity, revenue, expenses, and withdrawals. They are held in the CATEGORY table, described below:

COLUMN	DESCRIPTION
CATEGORY_ID	Category unique identifier
CATEGORY_DESC	Description of category
NORMAL_BALANCE	Side of the accounting equation
CLASS	Permanent / Temporary
INCREASE_JRNL_TYPE	Type of journal to increase balance (Normal Balance)
DECREASE_JRNL_TYPE	Type of journal to decrease balance (Normal Balance inverse)

Table 3.1 Category table description

A category's normal balance, dictated by its side of the accounting equation, indicates the type of journal to increase the balance and the inverse to decrease it. Though it is possible for an account with a debit normal balance to have a credit balance and vice versa, the situations should be rare.

Revenue, expenses, and withdrawals are classified temporary because they start each financial year from zero after application of their cumulative effects to equity. Assets, liabilities, and equity are classified permanent as they carry forward balances from one year to the next.

Table 3.2 lists the six categories, presenting a summary of double-entry rules.

CATEGORY_ID	CATEGORY_DESC	NORMAL_BALANCE	CLASS	INCREASE_JRNL_TYPE	DECREASE_JRNL_TYPE
1	Assets	Debit	Permanent	Debit	Credit
2	Liabilities	Credit	Permanent	Credit	Debit
3	Equity	Credit	Permanent	Credit	Debit
4	Revenue	Credit	Temporary	Credit	Debit
5	Expenses	Debit	Temporary	Debit	Credit
6	Withdrawals	Debit	Temporary	Debit	Credit

Table 3.2 List of categories

Types of accounts

Each category comprises specific types of accounts, described below:

- Assets

Type of account	Description
Current assets	Cash, cash equivalents, or convertible into cash within the next twelve months. They include cash on hand, cash in the bank, goods for resale, and debt owed by customers known as debtors.
Noncurrent assets	Assets acquired for productive use and not expected to be sold or converted into cash within the next twelve months. Examples include office equipment, office furniture, vehicles, buildings, and land.

- Liabilities

Type of account	Description
Current liabilities	Consist of money owing on goods and services and loans payable within the next twelve months. Examples include tax and money owing to suppliers of goods and services referred to as creditors.
Noncurrent liabilities	Comprise long-term loans not payable within the next twelve months. Examples include a mortgage.

- Equity

Type of account	Description
Capital	Owner's direct investment.

- Revenue

Type of account	Description
Operating revenue	Income from normal business activities of selling goods and services.
Other income	Revenue generated outside the normal operations of a business, e.g., interest earned.

- Expenses

Type of account	Description
Direct expenses	Costs incurred in generating revenue. They include cost of goods sold.
Operating expenses	Costs incurred to run a business. Examples include premises rental, staff salaries, and electricity.

- Withdrawals

Type of account	Description
Drawings	Resources withdrawn by the owner at the expense of equity.

Types of accounts are held in the ACCOUNT_TYPE table, defined below.

COLUMN	DESCRIPTION
ACCT_TYPE_ID	Account type unique identifier
ACCT_TYPE_DESC	Account type description
CATEGORY_ID	Category identifier
ACCT_ID_RANGE_START	First account id in the range allocated
ACCT_ID_RANGE_END	Last account id in the range allocated

Table 3.3 Account type table description

A range of accounts is allocated to each type of account to simplify data retrieval. An example of a listing from the table is shown below:

ACCT_TYPE_ID	ACCT_TYPE_DESC	CATEGORY_ID	ACCT_ID_RANGE_START	ACCT_ID_RANGE_END
1	Current assets	1	1000	1499
2	Non-current assets	1	1500	1999
3	Current liabilities	2	2000	2499
4	Non-current liabilities	2	2500	2999
5	Capital	3	3000	3999
6	Operational Income	4	4000	4499
7	Other Income	4	4500	4999
8	Direct expenses	5	5000	5199
9	Operational expenses	5	5200	5999
10	Drawings	6	6000	6099

Table 3.4 List of types of accounts

Chart of accounts

A chart of accounts is a complete list of accounts used in a business. It includes summary accounts that group related accounts for brevity in reporting.

The accounts receivable account summarises customer accounts (debtors) and reports the total debt in financial statements. Similarly, the accounts payable account groups suppliers of goods and services (creditors) to report the overall total owed in financial statements.

The following twenty-three accounts cater for the types of transactions anticipated and the level of detail required in reporting.

- Current assets

Account	Purpose
Cash	Record cash transactions and manage cash on hand
Bank	Manage the business bank account
Accounts receivable	Summarise debt owed by all customers (debtors)
TeeBee Vido Limited	Record sales, returns, and receipts from TeeBee Vido Limited
Tailspin & Mandown LLP	Record sales, returns, and receipts from Tailspin & Mandown LLP
Inventory	Maintain a record of inflows and outflows of goods for resale

- Noncurrent assets

Account	Purpose
Computer hardware	Manage computer hardware owned by the business
Office furniture	Manage office furniture owned

- Current liabilities

Account	Purpose
Accounts payable	Summarise credit due to suppliers (creditors) for goods or services
Toks Wholesalers	Record purchases, returns, and payments to Toks Wholesalers
Rafata Inc.	Record purchases, returns, and payments to Rafata Inc.

- Noncurrent liabilities

Account	Purpose
Bank loan	Manage bank loan transactions (borrowings and payments)

- Capital

Account	Purpose
Capital—D Kay	Manage owner's investment into the business

- Operational income

Account	Purpose
Sales	Record revenue from sales
Sales returns	Monitor sales returns

- Other income

Account	Purpose
Interest earned	Record interest revenue

- Direct expenses

Account	Purpose
Cost of sales	Record expense incurred to earn revenue

- Operational expenses

Account	Purpose
Salaries	Record salaries expense
Telephone and Internet	Record telephone and Internet expense
Gas and electricity	Record gas and electricity expense
Premises rental	Record premises rental expense
Advertising	Record advertising expense

- Drawings

Account	Purpose
Drawings—D Kay	Record withdrawals

Accounts are held in the ACCOUNT table, described below:

COLUMN	DESCRIPTION
ACCT_ID	Account unique identifier
ACCT_DESC	Description or name of account
ACCT_TYPE_ID	Account type identifier
SUMMARY_ACCT_ID	Summary account identifier

Table 3.5 Account table description

Account Id's of cash and cash equivalent accounts are held in the single-column table, CASH_ACCOUNT.

Figure 3.1 below models the relationship between chart of accounts tables.

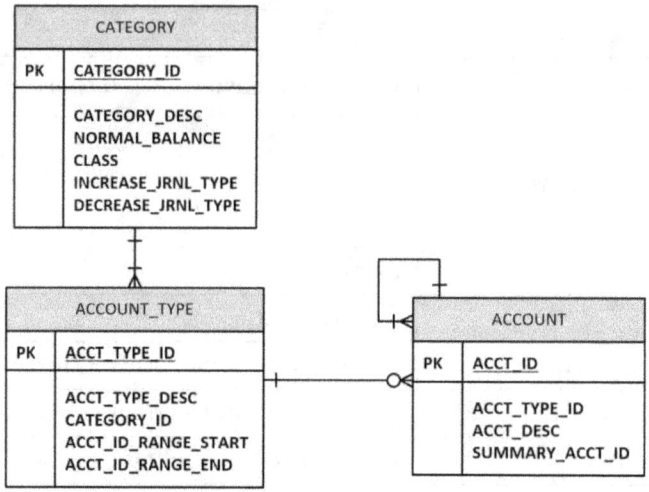

Figure 3.1 Chart of accounts tables relationships

The recursive relationship of the ACCOUNT enables grouping of related accounts.

The following TSQL code retrieves a sample chart of accounts from the database.

```
SELECT C.CATEGORY_ID, C.CATEGORY_DESC, T.ACCT_TYPE_ID,
T.ACCT_TYPE_DESC, A.ACCT_ID, A.ACCT_DESC, A.SUMMARY_ACCT_ID
FROM CATEGORY AS C
INNER JOIN ACCOUNT_TYPE AS T ON C.CATEGORY_ID =
T.CATEGORY_ID
INNER JOIN ACCOUNT AS A ON T.ACCT_TYPE_ID = A.ACCT_TYPE_ID
```

The result set in Table 3.7 lists accounts in sequential order of categories.

CATEGORY_ID	CATEGORY_DESC	ACCT_TYPE_ID	ACCT_TYPE_DESC	ACCT_ID	ACCT_DESC	SUMMARY_ACCT_ID
1	Assets	1	Current assets	1000	Cash	1000
1	Assets	1	Current assets	1010	Bank	1010
1	Assets	1	Current assets	1020	Accounts Receivable	1020
1	Assets	1	Current assets	1021	TeeBee Vido Limited	1020
1	Assets	1	Current assets	1022	Tailspin & Mandown LLP	1020
1	Assets	1	Current assets	1030	Inventory	1030
1	Assets	2	Non-current assets	1500	Computer Hardware	1500
1	Assets	2	Non-current assets	1520	Office Furniture	1520
2	Liabilities	3	Current liabilities	2000	Accounts Payable	2000
2	Liabilities	3	Current liabilities	2001	Toks Wholesalers	2000
2	Liabilities	3	Current liabilities	2002	Rafata Inc.	2000
2	Liabilities	4	Non-current liabilities	2500	Bank Loan	2500
3	Equity	5	Capital	3000	Capital - D Kay	3000
4	Revenue	6	Operational Income	4000	Sales	4000
4	Revenue	6	Operational Income	4010	Sales Returns	4010
4	Revenue	7	Other Income	4600	Interest Earned	4600
5	Expenses	8	Direct expenses	5000	Cost of Sales	5000
5	Expenses	9	Operational expenses	5200	Salaries	5200
5	Expenses	9	Operational expenses	5210	Telephone & Internet	5210
5	Expenses	9	Operational expenses	5220	Gas & Electricity	5220
5	Expenses	9	Operational expenses	5260	Premises Rental	5260
5	Expenses	9	Operational expenses	5270	Advertising	5270
6	Withdrawals	10	Drawings	6000	Drawings - D Kay	6000

Table 3.7 Chart of accounts list

A listing of the CASH_ACCOUNT table, below, shows pointers to the cash and the bank account.

ACCT_ID
1000
1010

Table 3.8 CASH_ACCOUNT table listing

Chapter 4: Fundamentals of Transactions

Activities

Transactions are the root of accounting data. They are classified into three broad activities: financing, investing, and operating. Each activity is associated with specific types of transactions.

Financing activities relate to the funding of a business. They are transactions with investors, the owner and lenders, such as the owner's direct investment, obtaining of long-term loans, withdrawals, and long-term loan repayments. The transactions primarily affect equity, withdrawals, and noncurrent liabilities.

Investing activities involve buying and disposal of resources a business needs to operate, expand, and grow. These resources are acquired for their productive use rather than resale. So, the transactions primarily impact noncurrent assets. Examples include purchase of office furniture and sale of obsolete office equipment.

Operating activities are the core activities a business engages in to make a profit and keep a business running. They affect current assets and current liabilities. Examples include buying and selling of goods and paying associated expenses.

Activities are held in the ACTIVITY table listed below:

ACTIVITY_ID	ACTIVITY_DESC
1	Operating
2	Investing
3	Financing

Table 4.1 List of activities

Examples of types of transactions under each activity are shown in Table 4.2.

Activity	Type of transaction
Financing	Owner investment
	Long term borrowing
	Withdrawal
	Long term loan payment
Investing	Purchase of non-current asset
	Sale of non-current asset
	Payment to non-current asset supplier
Operating	Sale
	Sale Returns
	Purchase of goods
	Purchase Returns
	Payment to goods supplier
	Customer Receipt
	Expense

Table 4.2 Types of transactions under each activity

Types of transactions

Each type of transaction primarily impacts an account of a specific category and has opposite effects on one or more accounts associated with potential methods of exchange.

A customer receipt, for instance, primarily impacts a customer (debtor) account, which is an asset. The other accounts impacted are determined by the mode of payment involving either cash or the bank, or a combination of both.

The following double-entry rules, held in the CATEGORY table, determine the types of journals to record the dual effects.

Category	To record	Type of journal
ASSET	Increase	Debit
	Decrease	Credit
LIABILITIES	Increase	Credit
	Decrease	Debit
EQUITY	Increase	Credit
	Decrease	Debit
REVENUE	Increase	Credit
	Decrease	Debit
EXPENSES	Increase	Debit
	Decrease	Credit
WITHDRAWALS	Increase	Debit
	Decrease	Credit

Table 4.3 Double-entry rules

Analysis of each of the following fourteen types of transactions uncovers the type of journals to record effects on accounts affected.

- Owner investment

Resources contributions into the business by the owner in either or a combination of cash, bank deposit, and tangible assets primarily increases equity, requiring a credit journal to record the effect. And the resultant increase in assets is recorded by debit journals, as summarised below.

PRIMARY ACCOUNT IMPACTED			POTENTIAL METHODS OF EXCHANGE			
Category	Effect	Type of Journal	Exchange method	Category	Effect	Type of Journal
Equity	Increase	Credit	Cash	Assets	Increase	Debit
			Bank	Assets	Increase	Debit
			Non-cash asset	Assets	Increase	Debit

Table 4.4 Owner investment transaction analysis

- Long-term borrowing

Long-term borrowing mainly increases liabilities and requires a credit journal to record the effect. The subsequent increase in assets is recorded by a debit journal, as shown below:

PRIMARY ACCOUNT IMPACTED			POTENTIAL METHODS OF EXCHANGE			
Category	Effect	Type of Journal	Exchange method	Category	Effect	Type of Journal
Liabilities	Increase	Credit	Cash	Assets	Increase	Debit
			Bank	Assets	Increase	Debit
			Non-cash asset	Assets	Increase	Debit

Table 4.5 Loan transaction analysis

- Withdrawal

Withdrawal of resources for personal use by the owner (in cash, goods, etc.) primarily increases withdrawals, which requires a debit journal to record the impact. A credit journal records the resultant decrease in assets, as shown below:

PRIMARY ACCOUNT IMPACTED			POTENTIAL METHODS OF EXCHANGE			
Category	Effect	Type of Journal	Exchange method	Category	Effect	Type of Journal
Withdrawals	Increase	Debit	Cash	Assets	Decrease	Credit
			Bank	Assets	Decrease	Credit
			Non-cash asset	Assets	Decrease	Credit

Table 4.6 Withdrawal transaction analysis

- Loan payment

A loan payment primarily reduces liabilities and requires a debit journal to record the effect. The compensating decrease in assets is recorded by a credit journal, as shown below:

PRIMARY ACCOUNT IMPACTED			POTENTIAL METHODS OF EXCHANGE			
Category	Effect	Type of Journal	Exchange method	Category	Effect	Type of Journal
Liabilities	Decrease	Credit	Cash	Assets	Decrease	Debit
			Bank	Assets	Decrease	Debit

Table 4.7 Loan payment transaction analysis

- Purchase of noncurrent asset

Purchase of a noncurrent asset principally increases assets and requires a debit journal to record the impact. The compensating decrease in assets or increase in liabilities is recorded by a credit journal, as shown below:

PRIMARY ACCOUNT IMPACTED			POTENTIAL METHODS OF EXCHANGE			
Category	Effect	Type of Journal	Exchange method	Category	Effect	Type of Journal
Assets	Increase	Debit	Cash	Assets	Decrease	Credit
			Bank	Assets	Decrease	Credit
			Credit	Liabilities	Increase	Credit

Table 4.8 Non-current asset purchase transaction analysis

- Sale of noncurrent asset

Sale of a noncurrent asset primarily decreases assets and requires a credit journal to record the effect. The corresponding increase in assets is recorded by a debit journal, as summarised below:

PRIMARY ACCOUNT IMPACTED			POTENTIAL METHODS OF EXCHANGE			
Category	Effect	Type of Journal	Exchange method	Category	Effect	Type of Journal
Assets	Decrease	Credit	Cash	Assets	Increase	Debit
			Bank	Assets	Increase	Debit
			Credit	Assets	Increase	Debit

Table 4.9 Non-current asset sale transaction analysis

- Payment to noncurrent asset supplier

A payment to a noncurrent asset supplier mainly decreases liabilities and requires a debit journal to record the effect. The corresponding decrease in assets is recorded by a credit journal, as summarised below:

PRIMARY ACCOUNT IMPACTED			POTENTIAL METHODS OF EXCHANGE			
Category	Effect	Type of Journal	Exchange method	Category	Effect	Type of Journal
Liabilities	Decrease	Debit	Cash	Assets	Decrease	Credit
			Bank	Assets	Decrease	Credit

Table 4.10 Payment to supplier transaction analysis

- Purchase of goods

Purchase of goods for resale primarily increases assets and requires a debit journal to record the effect. The compensating decrease in assets or increase in liabilities is recorded by a credit journal, as summed up below:

PRIMARY ACCOUNT IMPACTED			POTENTIAL METHODS OF EXCHANGE			
Category	Effect	Type of Journal	Exchange method	Category	Effect	Type of Journal
Assets	Increase	Debit	Cash	Assets	Decrease	Credit
			Bank	Assets	Decrease	Credit
			Credit	Liabilities	Increase	Credit

Table 4.11 Purchase of goods transaction analysis

- Return of goods purchased

Outward return of goods to suppliers principally decreases assets and requires a credit journal to record the impact. The compensating increase in assets or decrease in liabilities is recorded by a debit journal, as summed up below:

PRIMARY ACCOUNT IMPACTED			POTENTIAL METHODS OF EXCHANGE			
Category	Effect	Type of Journal	Exchange method	Category	Effect	Type of Journal
Assets	Decrease	Credit	Cash	Assets	Decrease	Debit
			Bank	Assets	Decrease	Debit
			Credit	Liabilities	Increase	Debit

Table 4.12 Purchase returns transaction analysis

- Payment to goods supplier

Payment to a goods supplier primarily decreases liabilities and requires a debit journal to record the effect. The corresponding decrease in assets is recorded by a credit journal.

PRIMARY ACCOUNT IMPACTED			POTENTIAL METHODS OF EXCHANGE			
Category	Effect	Type of Journal	Exchange method	Category	Effect	Type of Journal
Liabilities	Decrease	Debit	Cash	Assets	Decrease	Credit
			Bank	Assets	Decrease	Credit

Table 4.13 Payment to goods supplier transaction analysis

- Sale of goods

A sale of goods primarily increases revenue and requires a credit journal to record the effect. The complementary increase in assets is recorded by a debit journal, as summed up below:

PRIMARY ACCOUNT IMPACTED			POTENTIAL METHODS OF EXCHANGE			
Category	Effect	Type of Journal	Exchange method	Category	Effect	Type of Journal
Revenue	Increase	Credit	Cash	Assets	Increase	Debit
			Bank	Assets	Increase	Debit
			Credit	Assets	Decrease	Debit

Table 4.14.1 Sale transaction analysis

A sale also triggers a decrease in inventory, which represents an expense of goods sold. The increase in expenses is recorded by a debit journal, and the corresponding decrease in assets is recorded by a credit journal, as shown below:

COST OF GOODS SOLD			CHANGE IN INVENTORY		
Category	Effect	Type of Journal	Category	Effect	Type of Journal
Expenses	Increase	Debit	Assets	Decrease	Credit

Table 4.14.2 Additional sale transaction analysis

- Sale returns

Inward return of goods sold primarily decreases revenue and requires a debit journal to record the effect. The corresponding decrease in assets is recorded by a credit journal, as summarised below:

PRIMARY ACCOUNT IMPACTED			POTENTIAL METHODS OF EXCHANGE			
Category	Effect	Type of Journal	Exchange method	Category	Effect	Type of Journal
Revenue	Decrease	Debit	Cash	Assets	Increase	Credit
			Bank	Assets	Increase	Credit
			Credit	Assets	Decrease	Credit

Table 4.15.1 Sale returns transaction analysis

Inward return of sold goods recovers expenses, which requires a credit journal to record the effect. The corresponding increase in assets is recorded by a debit journal, as shown below:

COST OF GOODS SOLD			CHANGE IN INVENTORY		
Category	Effect	Type of Journal	Category	Effect	Type of Journal
Expenses	Decrease	Credit	Assets	Increase	Debit

Table 4.15.2 Additional sale returns transaction analysis

- Customer receipt

A customer receipt primarily decreases accounts receivable assets and requires a credit journal to record the effect. The corresponding increase in assets is recorded by a debit journal, as summarised below:

PRIMARY ACCOUNT IMPACTED			POTENTIAL METHODS OF EXCHANGE			
Category	Effect	Type of Journal	Exchange method	Category	Effect	Type of Journal
Assets	Decrease	Credit	Cash	Assets	Increase	Debit
			Bank	Assets	Increase	Debit

Table 4.16 Customer receipt transaction analysis

- Expense

An expense primarily increases expenses and requires a debit journal to record its effect. The resultant decrease in assets or increase in liabilities is recorded by a credit journal, as shown below.

PRIMARY ACCOUNT IMPACTED			POTENTIAL METHODS OF EXCHANGE			
Category	Effect	Type of Journal	Exchange method	Category	Effect	Type of Journal
Expenses	Increase	Debit	Cash	Assets	Decrease	Credit
			Bank	Assets	Decrease	Credit
			Credit	Liabilities	Increase	Credit

Table 4.17 Expense transaction analysis

Storage of preanalysis

Types of transactions and details of the primary accounts impacted are held in the TRANS_TYPE table, described below:

COLUMN	DESCRIPTION
TRANS_TYPE_ID	Transaction type unique identifier
TRANS_TYPE_DESC	Transaction description
ACTIVITY_ID	Activity identifier
CATEGORY_ID	Category identifier of primary account impacted
EFFECT	Effect on balance of account (increase or decrease)
JRNL_TYPE	Journal type based on category and effect (debit / credit)

Table 4.18 TRANS_TYPE table description

Potential methods of exchange for each type of transaction are held in the TRANS_TYPE_MOE table, described below:

COLUMN	DESCRIPTION
TRANS_TYPE_MOE_ID	Unique identifier
TRANS_TYPE_ID	Transaction Type Identifier
MOE_ID	Method of exchange identifier
CATEGORY_ID	Category identifier
EFFECT	Increase or Decrease
JRNL_TYPE	Journal type based on category and effect (debit / credit)

Table 4.19 TRANS_TYPE_MOE table description

Cost of sales, only applicable to sales, and sales returns are held in the TRANS_TYPE_COS table, described below:

COLUMN	DESCRIPTION
TRANS_TYPE_ID	Transaction type identifier
CATEGORY_ID	Primary account category identifier
EFFECT	Effect on balance account (increase or decrease)
ACTION	Journal type based on category and effect (debit / credit)

Table 4.20 TRANS_TYPE_COS table description

Changes to inventory from sales and sales returns are held in the TRANS_TYPE_INV_CHANGE table, described below:

COLUMN	DESCRIPTION
TRANS_TYPE_ID	Transaction type identifier
CATEGORY_ID	Primary account category identifier
EFFECT	Effect on balance account (increase or decrease)
ACTION	Journal type based on category and effect (debit / credit)

Table 4.21 TRANS_TYPE_INV_CHANGE table description

The four data stores are used as decision tables to indicate types of journals for every combination of variables.

Table 4.22 lists the TRANS_TYPE table containing fourteen types of transactions anticipated, each showing the category of the primary account affected and the type of journal to record the effect.

TRANS_TYPE_ID	TRANS_TYPE_DESC	ACTIVITY_DESC	CATEGORY_ID	CATEGORY_DESC	EFFECT	ACTION
1	Sale	Operating	4	Revenue	Increase	Credit
2	Sale Returns	Operating	4	Revenue	Decrease	Debit
3	Purchase of goods	Operating	1	Assets	Increase	Debit
4	Purchase returns	Operating	1	Assets	Decrease	Credit
5	Payment to goods supplier	Operating	2	Liabilities	Decrease	Debit
6	Customer receipt	Operating	1	Assets	Decrease	Credit
7	Expense	Operating	5	Expenses	Increase	Debit
8	Purchase of non-current asset	Investing	1	Assets	Increase	Debit
9	Disposal of non-current asset	Investing	1	Assets	Decrease	Credit
10	Payment to non-current asset supplier	Investing	2	Liabilities	Decrease	Debit
11	Owner investment	Financing	3	Equity	Increase	Credit
12	Long term borrowing	Financing	2	Liabilities	Increase	Credit
13	Withdrawal	Financing	6	Withdrawals	Increase	Debit
14	Long term debt payment	Financing	2	Liabilities	Decrease	Debit

Table 4.22 List of types of transactions

Potential methods of exchange for financing activities are listed from the TRANS_TYPE_MOE table, below:

TRANS_TYPE_MOE_ID	TRANS_TYPE_ID	MOE_ID	CATEGORY_ID	EFFECT	JRNL_TYPE
28	11	1	1	Increase	Debit
29	11	2	1	Increase	Debit
30	11	4	1	Increase	Debit
31	12	1	1	Increase	Debit
32	12	2	1	Increase	Debit
33	12	4	1	Increase	Debit
34	13	1	1	Decrease	Credit
35	13	2	1	Decrease	Credit
36	13	4	1	Decrease	Credit
37	14	1	1	Decrease	Credit
38	14	2	1	Decrease	Credit

Table 4.23 Potential methods of exchange for financing activities

Table 4.24 lists potential methods of exchange for investing activities.

TRANS_TYPE_MOE_ID	TRANS_TYPE_ID	MOE_ID	CATEGORY_ID	EFFECT	JRNL_TYPE
20	8	1	1	Decrease	Credit
21	8	2	1	Decrease	Credit
22	8	3	2	Increase	Credit
23	9	1	1	Increase	Debit
24	9	2	1	Increase	Debit
25	9	3	1	Increase	Debit
26	10	1	1	Decrease	Credit
27	10	2	1	Decrease	Credit

Table 4.24 Potential methods of exchange for investing activities

Table 4.25 lists potential methods of exchange for operating activities.

TRANS_TYPE_MOE_ID	TRANS_TYPE_ID	MOE_ID	CATEGORY_ID	EFFECT	JRNL_TYPE
1	1	1	1	Increase	Debit
2	1	2	1	Increase	Debit
3	1	3	1	Increase	Debit
4	2	1	1	Decrease	Credit
5	2	2	1	Decrease	Credit
6	2	3	1	Decrease	Credit
7	3	1	1	Decrease	Credit
8	3	2	1	Decrease	Credit
9	3	3	2	Increase	Credit
10	4	1	1	Increase	Debit
11	4	2	1	Increase	Debit
12	4	3	2	Decrease	Debit
13	5	1	1	Decrease	Credit
14	5	2	1	Decrease	Credit
15	6	1	1	Increase	Debit
16	6	2	1	Increase	Debit
17	7	1	1	Decrease	Credit
18	7	2	1	Decrease	Credit
19	7	3	2	Increase	Credit

Table 4.25 Potential methods of exchange for operating activities

Listed below, from the TRANS_TYPE_COS table, are costs of sales pertaining to two types of transactions—sales and sales returns.

TRANS_TYPE_ID	CATEGORY_ID	EFFECT	JRNL_TYPE
1	5	Increase	Debit
2	5	Decrease	Credit

Table 4.26 Cost of sales

Changes to inventory caused by sales and sales returns, held in the TRANS_TYPE_INV_CHANGE table, are listed below.

TRANS_TYPE_ID	CATEGORY_ID	EFFECT	JRNL_TYPE
1	1	Decrease	Debit
2	1	Increase	Credit

Table 4.27 Change to inventory

Transaction data store

Transaction data comprise the following components:

(a) Main transaction details, such as the type of transaction, description, date, amount, and so on.
(b) Combination of methods of exchange used in the transaction.
(c) Cost of sales expense, where applicable.
(d) Change to inventory triggered by either a sale or sale return.

The main transaction details are held in the TRANS table, described below:

COLUMN	DESCRIPTION
TRANS_ID	Transaction unique identifier
TRANS_TYPE_ID	Transaction type identifier
TRANS_DATE	Date of transaction
MONTH_ID	Financial month identifier
TRANS_DESC	Transaction description
AMOUNT	Transaction amount
ACCT_ID	Identifier of primary account affected

Table 4.28 TRANS table description

Methods of exchange pertaining to each transaction are held in the TRANS_MOE table, described below:

COLUMN	DESCRIPTION
TRANS_MOE_ID	Unique identifier
TRANS_ID	Transaction identifier
MOE_ID	Method of exchange identifier
AMOUNT	Amount value
ACCT_ID	Identifier of account associated with method of exchange

Table 4.29 TRANS_MOE table description

A transaction may have multiple rows in the table, each representing the amount and method of exchange employed.

Cost of sales expenses for sales and sales returns are held in the TRANS_COS table, described below:

COLUMN	DESCRIPTION
TRANS_COS_ID	Unique identifier
TRANS_ID	Transaction identifier
AMOUNT	Cost of goods sold amount value
ACCT_ID	Identifier of expenses account

Table 4.30 TRANS_COS table description

Changes to inventory triggered by sales and sales returns are held in the TRANS_INV_CHANGE table, described below:

COLUMN	DESCRIPTION
TRANS_INV_CHANGE_ID	Unique identifier
TRANS_ID	Transaction identifier
AMOUNT	Amount value of inventory
ACCOUNT_ID	Identifier of inventory account

Table 4.31 TRANS_INV_CHANGE table description

Each of the four tables that hold transaction data is used to generate journal entries based on variables in the related decision table shown in Table 4.32:

TRANSACTION TABLE	RELATED DECISION TABLE
TRANS	TRANS_TYPE
TRANS_MOE	TRANS_TYPE_MOE
TRANS_COS	TRANS_TYPE_COS
TRANS_INV_CHANGE	TRANS_TYPE_INV_CHANGE

Table 4.32 Transaction and related decision table

Figure 4.1 models the relationships between the tables used to generate journals entries.

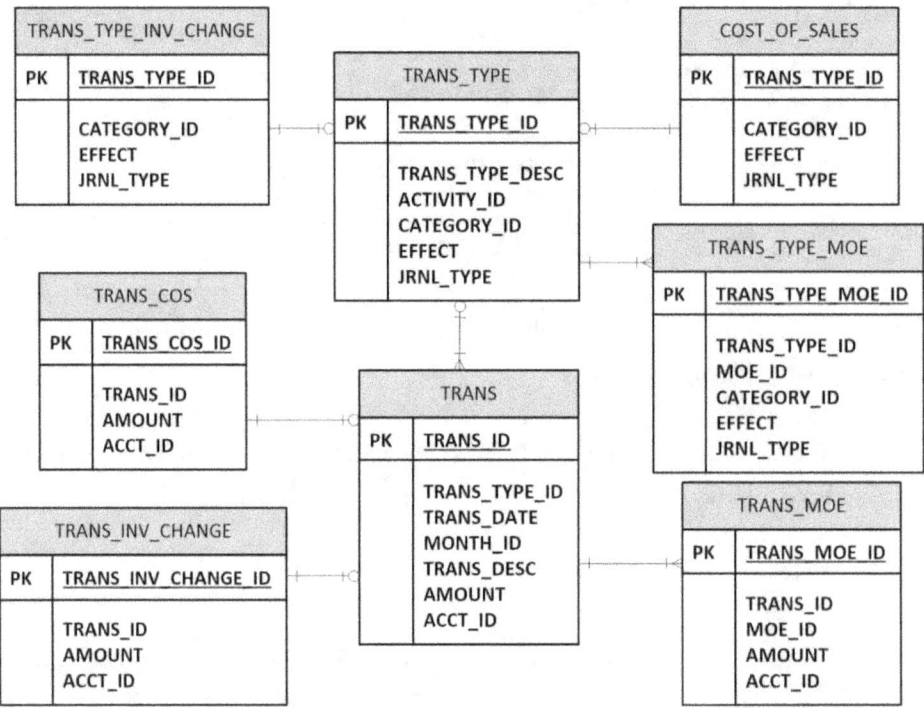

Figure 4.1 Journal entries data source tables

Accounting data store

A minimum of two journal entries, a debit and a credit, are generated for every transaction and stored in the JOURNAL table, described below:

COLUMN	DESCRIPTION
JOURNAL_ID	Unique identifier
TRANS_ID	Transaction Identifier
JOURNAL_DATE	Date of journal
MONTH_ID	Month Identifier
ACCT_ID	Account Identifier
NOTES	Justification of journal
DEBIT	Debit amount (if any)
CREDIT	Credit Amount (if any)
DEBIT_BALANCE	Running Debit Balance (if any)
CREDIT_BALANCE	Running Credit Balance (if any)

Table 4.33 JOURNAL table description

The debit and credit values are always held as positive numbers and so are the resultant debit or credit balances.

The LEDGER table, described in Table 4.34, contains up-to-date monthly summaries of each account.

COLUMN	DESCRIPTION
LEDGER_ID	Unique identifier
MONTH_ID	Month Identifier
ACCT_ID	Account Identifier
DEBIT	Debit amount total for the month
CREDIT	Credit amount total for the month
DEBIT_BALANCE	Running Debit Balance (if any)
CREDIT_BALANCE	Running Credit Balance (if any)

Table 4.34 LEDGER table description

A record of an account in the LEDGER table is an aggregate of related multiple entries for the month in the JOURNAL table.

Chapter 5: Transaction Processing

Integrated process

Integrated transaction processing encompasses recording transaction details, trigger immediate generation of journal entries, and activate updates to the ledger. The process employs decision tables to direct processing and build accounting data as a background task. Running balances of accounts affected are calculated from values obtained from the ledger.

The following business events in month 201601 illustrate transaction recording and processing:

(a) On January 2, 2016, D Kay started a business with a £15,000 deposit into the bank account.

The type of transaction is owner investment, which primarily impacts the capital account. Drawing reference details from the TRANS_TYPE and ACCOUNT tables, the transaction is recorded in the TRANS table as

TRANS						
TRANS_ID	TRANS_TYPE_ID	TRANS_DATE	MONTH_ID	TRANS_DESC	AMOUNT	ACCT_ID
1	11	02-Jan-16	201601	Business start-up investment by owner	15000.00	3000

TRANS_TYPE	
TRANS_TYPE_ID	TRANS_TYPE_DESC
11	Owner investment

ACCOUNT	
ACCT_ID	ACCT_DESC
3000	Capital - D Kay

Transaction 5.1.1 Owner investment

And the bank deposit, the means of resources exchange, is recorded in the TRANS_MOE table as follows:

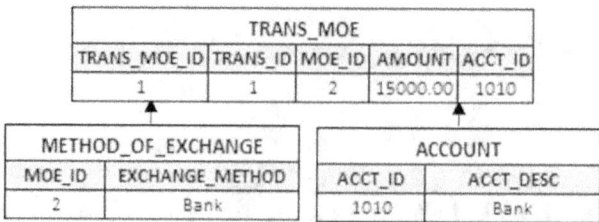

Transaction 5.1.2 Bank deposit

The following two journal entries are generated:

- Capital account increase

Journal-entry details to record effects to the capital account are drawn from transaction details held in the TRANS and TRANS_TYPE tables, as shown below:

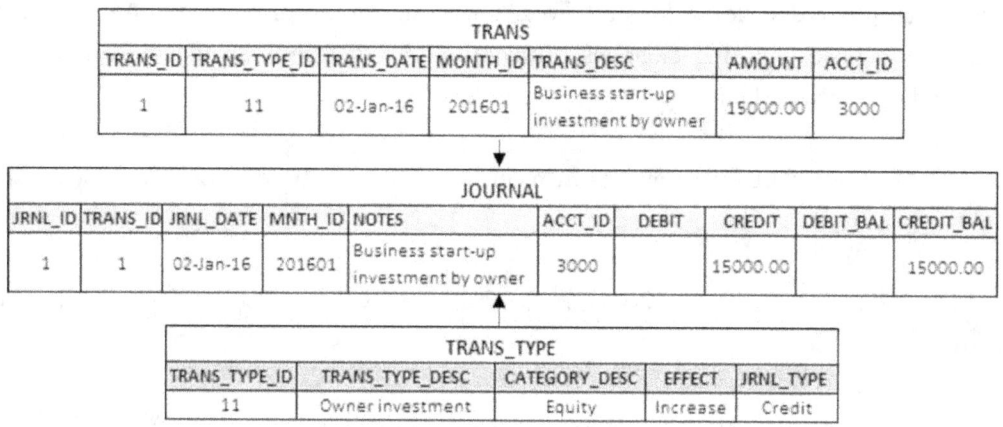

Transaction 5.1.3 Capital increase journal

The running balance is the same as the transaction value as this is the first transaction that impacts the account.

- Bank account increase

The opposite journal entry that records effects to the bank account draws narrative details from the TRANS table, account details from the TRANS_MOE table, and the type of journal from the TRANS_TYPE_MOE table, as shown below:

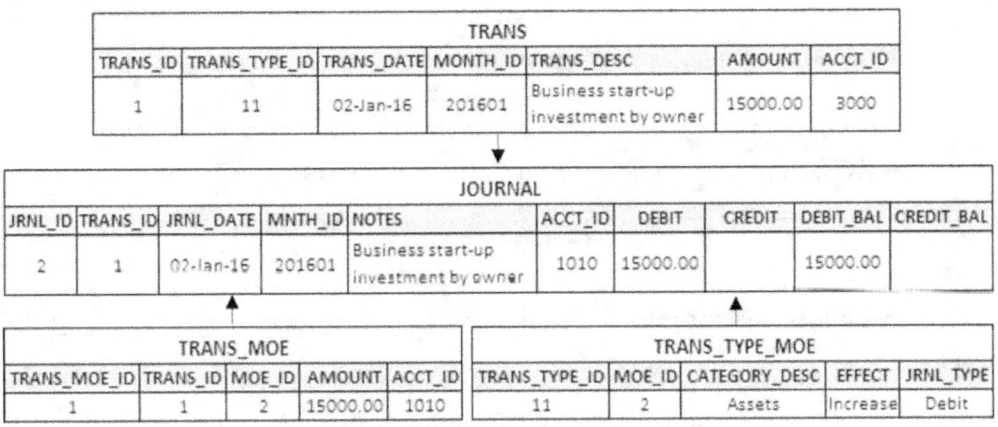

Transaction 5.1.4 Bank increase journal

The two journal entries for the transaction indicate that the amount debited is equal to the amount credited, and the overall credit balance is identical to the debit balance.

JOURNAL									
JRNL_ID	TRANS_ID	JRNL_DATE	MNTH_ID	NOTES	ACCT_ID	DEBIT	CREDIT	DEBIT_BAL	CREDIT_BAL
1	1	02-Jan-16	201601	Business start-up investment by owner	3000		15000.00		15000.00
2	1	02-Jan-16	201601	Business start-up investment by owner	1010	15000.00		15000.00	

Transaction 5.1.5 Owner investment transaction journal entries

Finally, a summary record for the month for each account is created in the ledger as

LEDGER						
LEDGER_ID	ACCT_ID	MNTH_ID	DEBIT	CREDIT	DEBIT_BAL	CREDIT_BAL
1	3000	201601		15000.00		1500.00
2	1010	201601	15000.00		15000.00	

Transaction 5.1.6 Capital and bank account summaries for the month

(b) On January 3, 2016, a five-year loan of £30,000 is granted by the bank and paid into the business bank account.

The transaction is categorised long-term borrowing and bank loan selected as the primary account affected. Transaction details are recorded in the TRANS table as

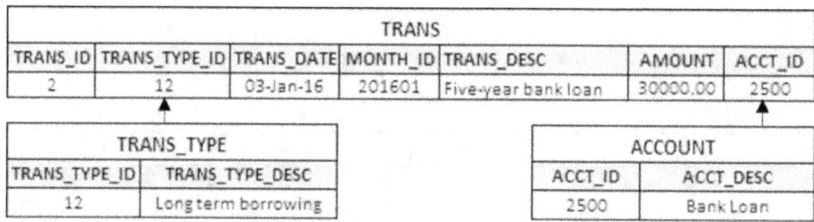

Transaction 5.2.1 Long term loan

The bank loan receipt into the bank account is recorded in the TRANS_MOE table as

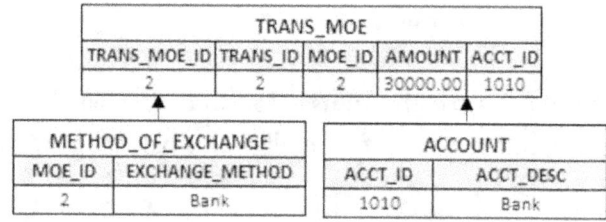

Transaction 5.2.2 Bank loan receipt

The following two journal entries are generated:

- Loan account increase

Journal entry details to record increase in liabilities are drawn from the TRANS and TRANS_TYPE tables as shown below:

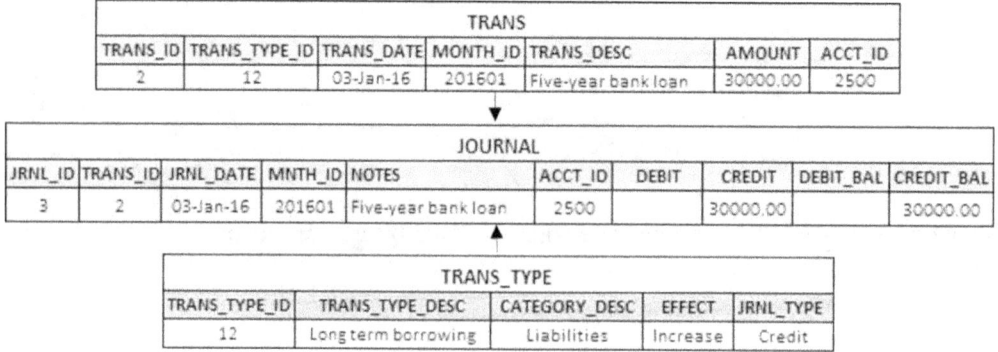

Transaction 5.2.3 Loan increase journal

- Bank account increase

The opposite journal that records an increase in the bank account is generated from details held in the tables TRANS, TRANS_MOE, and TRANS_TYPE_MOE as shown below:

TRANS						
TRANS_ID	TRANS_TYPE_ID	TRANS_DATE	MONTH_ID	TRANS_DESC	AMOUNT	ACCT_ID
2	12	03-Jan-16	201601	Five-year bank loan	30000.00	2500

JOURNAL									
JRNL_ID	TRANS_ID	JRNL_DATE	MNTH_ID	NOTES	ACCT_ID	DEBIT	CREDIT	DEBIT_BAL	CREDIT_BAL
4	2	03-Jan-16	201601	Five-year bank loan	1010	30000.00		45000.00	

TRANS_MOE				
TRANS_MOE_ID	TRANS_ID	MOE_ID	AMOUNT	ACCT_ID
2	2	2	30000.00	1010

TRANS_TYPE_MOE				
TRANS_TYPE_ID	MOE_ID	CATEGORY_DESC	EFFECT	JRNL_TYPE
12	2	Assets	Increase	Debit

Transaction 5.2.4 Bank increase journal

The running balance of the bank account is increased by the value of the loan. So, the month's summary details for the bank account are updated, and a record for the loan account is created in the ledger as follows:

LEDGER						
LEDGER_ID	ACCT_ID	MNTH_ID	DEBIT	CREDIT	DEBIT_BAL	CREDIT_BAL
2	1010	201601	45000.00		45000.00	
3	2500	201601		30000.00		30000.00

Transaction 5.2.5 Loan and bank summaries for the month

(c) On the 3rd January 2016, £1 000 is paid by cheque for premises rental.

The expense transaction, which primarily impacts the premises rental account, is recorded in the TRANS table as

TRANS						
TRANS_ID	TRANS_TYPE_ID	TRANS_DATE	MONTH_ID	TRANS_DESC	AMOUNT	ACCT_ID
3	7	03-Jan-16	201601	Premises rental	1000.00	5260

TRANS_TYPE	
TRANS_TYPE_ID	TRANS_TYPE_DESC
7	Expense

ACCOUNT	
ACCT_ID	ACCT_DESC
5260	Premises Rental

Transaction 5.3.1 Premises rental expense

The payment by cheque is stored in the TRANS_MOE table as

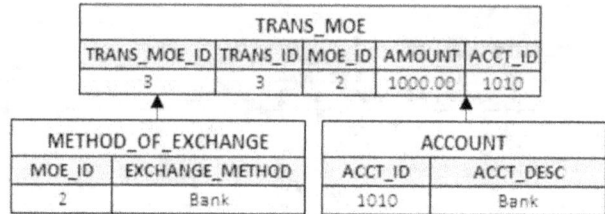

TRANS_MOE				
TRANS_MOE_ID	TRANS_ID	MOE_ID	AMOUNT	ACCT_ID
3	3	2	1000.00	1010

METHOD_OF_EXCHANGE	
MOE_ID	EXCHANGE_METHOD
2	Bank

ACCOUNT	
ACCT_ID	ACCT_DESC
1010	Bank

Transaction 5.3.2 Premises rental payment

The following two journal entries are generated:

- Increase in rental expense

Journal entry details to record increase in the balance of the premises rental account are stored as:

TRANS						
TRANS_ID	TRANS_TYPE_ID	TRANS_DATE	MONTH_ID	TRANS_DESC	AMOUNT	ACCT_ID
3	7	03-Jan-16	201601	Premises rental	1000.00	5260

JOURNAL									
JRNL_ID	TRANS_ID	JRNL_DATE	MNTH_ID	NOTES	ACCT_ID	DEBIT	CREDIT	DEBIT_BAL	CREDIT_BAL
5	3	03-Jan-16	201601	Premises rental	5260	1000.00		1000.00	

TRANS_TYPE				
TRANS_TYPE_ID	TRANS_TYPE_DESC	CATEGORY_DESC	EFFECT	JRNL_TYPE
7	Expense	Expenses	Increase	Debit

Transaction 5.3.3 Premises rental expense

- Decrease in bank account

The opposite journal entry that records a corresponding decrease in the balance of the bank account is stored as

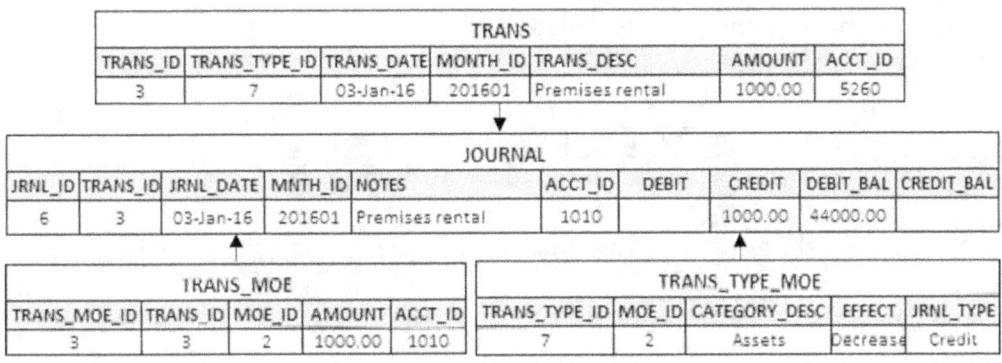

Transaction 5.3.4 Bank account decrease journal

The month's summary details of the bank account are updated, and a premises rental account is created in the ledger as follows:

LEDGER						
LEDGER_ID	ACCT_ID	MNTH_ID	DEBIT	CREDIT	DEBIT_BAL	CREDIT_BAL
2	1010	201601	45000.00	1000.00	44000.00	
4	5260	201601	1000.00		1000.00	

Transaction 5.3.5 Bank and premises rental summaries for the month

(d) On January 4, office furniture is bought for £4,500 and paid for by cheque.

The transaction, regarded as a purchase of a noncurrent asset primarily affecting the office furniture account, is recorded as

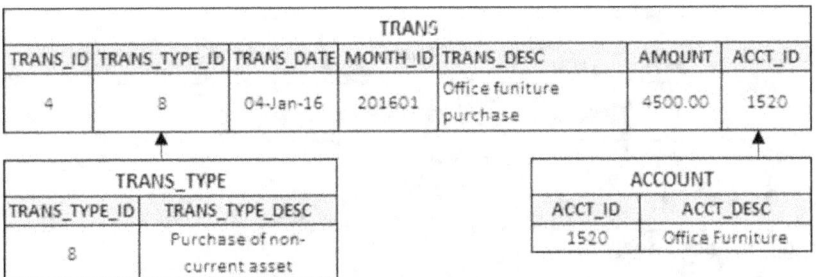

Transaction 5.4.1 Purchase of non-current assets

The payment by cheque is recorded as

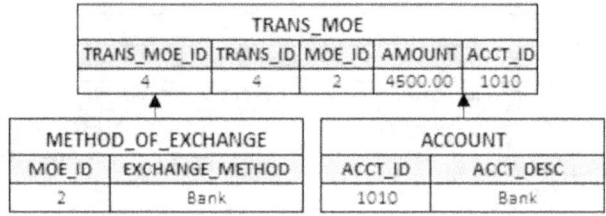

TRANS_MOE				
TRANS_MOE_ID	TRANS_ID	MOE_ID	AMOUNT	ACCT_ID
4	4	2	4500.00	1010

METHOD_OF_EXCHANGE	
MOE_ID	EXCHANGE_METHOD
2	Bank

ACCOUNT	
ACCT_ID	ACCT_DESC
1010	Bank

Transaction 5.4.2 Payment for office furniture

The following two journal entries are generated:

- Increase in office furniture

Journal entry details to record increase in the balance of the office furniture account are stored as

TRANS						
TRANS_ID	TRANS_TYPE_ID	TRANS_DATE	MONTH_ID	TRANS_DESC	AMOUNT	ACCT_ID
4	8	04-Jan-16	201601	Office funiture purchase	4500.00	1520

JOURNAL									
JRNL_ID	TRANS_ID	JRNL_DATE	MNTH_ID	NOTES	ACCT_ID	DEBIT	CREDIT	DEBIT_BAL	CREDIT_BAL
7	4	04-Jan-16	201601	Office funiture purchase	1520	4500.00		4500.00	

TRANS_TYPE				
TRANS_TYPE_ID	TRANS_TYPE_DESC	CATEGORY_DESC	EFFECT	JRNL_TYPE
8	Purchase of non-current asset	Assets	Increase	Debit

Transaction 5.4.3 Office furniture journal

- Decrease in bank account

The opposite journal entry that records a corresponding decrease in the balance of the bank account is stored as

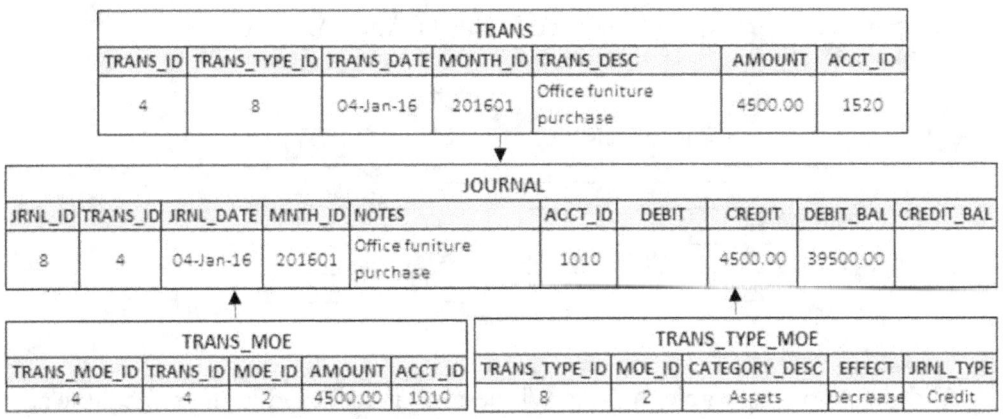

TRANS						
TRANS_ID	TRANS_TYPE_ID	TRANS_DATE	MONTH_ID	TRANS_DESC	AMOUNT	ACCT_ID
4	8	04-Jan-16	201601	Office funiture purchase	4500.00	1520

JOURNAL									
JRNL_ID	TRANS_ID	JRNL_DATE	MNTH_ID	NOTES	ACCT_ID	DEBIT	CREDIT	DEBIT_BAL	CREDIT_BAL
8	4	04-Jan-16	201601	Office funiture purchase	1010		4500.00	39500.00	

TRANS_MOE				
TRANS_MOE_ID	TRANS_ID	MOE_ID	AMOUNT	ACCT_ID
4	4	2	4500.00	1010

TRANS_TYPE_MOE				
TRANS_TYPE_ID	MOE_ID	CATEGORY_DESC	EFFECT	JRNL_TYPE
8	2	Assets	Decrease	Credit

Transaction 5.4.4 Bank account decrease journal

The month's summary for the bank account is updated, and a summary record for office furniture account created in the ledger as

LEDGER						
LEDGER_ID	ACCT_ID	MNTH_ID	DEBIT	CREDIT	DEBIT_BAL	CREDIT_BAL
2	1010	201601	45000.00	5500.00	39500.00	
5	1520	201601	4500.00		4500.00	

Transaction 5.4.5 Bank and office furniture summaries

(e) On January 6, three hundred cartridges were bought for resale for £30 each from Toks Wholesalers, paying £2,000 by cheque upfront and the balance of £7,000 payable in sixty days.

The transaction is recognised as a purchase of goods, which primarily impacts the inventory account. It is recorded as

TRANS						
TRANS_ID	TRANS_TYPE_ID	TRANS_DATE	MONTH_ID	TRANS_DESC	AMOUNT	ACCT_ID
5	3	06-Jan-16	201601	Purchase of 300 cartridges @£30 each	9000.00	1030

TRANS_TYPE	
TRANS_TYPE_ID	TRANS_TYPE_DESC
3	Purchase of goods

ACCOUNT	
ACCT_ID	ACCT_DESC
1030	Inventory

Transaction 5.5.1 Purchase of goods for resale

The payment by cheque is recorded in the TRANS_MOE tables as

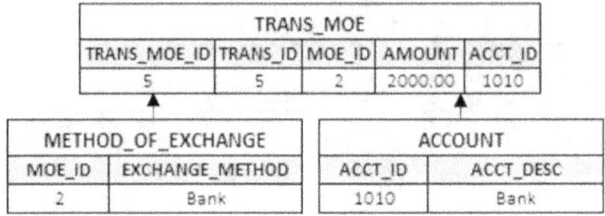

TRANS_MOE				
TRANS_MOE_ID	TRANS_ID	MOE_ID	AMOUNT	ACCT_ID
5	5	2	2000.00	1010

METHOD_OF_EXCHANGE	
MOE_ID	EXCHANGE_METHOD
2	Bank

ACCOUNT	
ACCT_ID	ACCT_DESC
1010	Bank

Transaction 5.5.2 Part payment to goods supplier

And the amount payable to Toks Wholesalers is recorded in the same table as

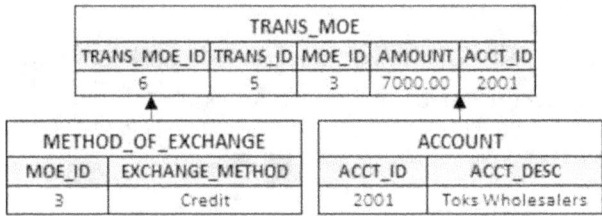

TRANS_MOE				
TRANS_MOE_ID	TRANS_ID	MOE_ID	AMOUNT	ACCT_ID
6	5	3	7000.00	2001

METHOD_OF_EXCHANGE	
MOE_ID	EXCHANGE_METHOD
3	Credit

ACCOUNT	
ACCT_ID	ACCT_DESC
2001	Toks Wholesalers

Transaction 5.5.3 Balance payable to goods supplier

The following three journal entries are generated:

- Increase in inventory

The increase in inventory is recorded as

TRANS						
TRANS_ID	TRANS_TYPE_ID	TRANS_DATE	MONTH_ID	TRANS_DESC	AMOUNT	ACCT_ID
5	3	06-Jan-16	201601	Purchase of 300 cartridges @£30 each	9000.00	1030

JOURNAL									
JRNL_ID	TRANS_ID	JRNL_DATE	MNTH_ID	NOTES	ACCT_ID	DEBIT	CREDIT	DEBIT_BAL	CREDIT_BAL
9	5	06-Jan-16	201601	Purchase of 300 cartridges @£30 each	1030	9000.00		9000.00	

TRANS_TYPE				
TRANS_TYPE_ID	TRANS_TYPE_DESC	CATEGORY_DESC	EFFECT	JRNL_TYPE
3	Purchase of goods	Assets	Increase	Debit

Transaction 5.5.4 Inventory increase journal

- Decrease in bank account

The decrease in the balance of the bank account is stored as

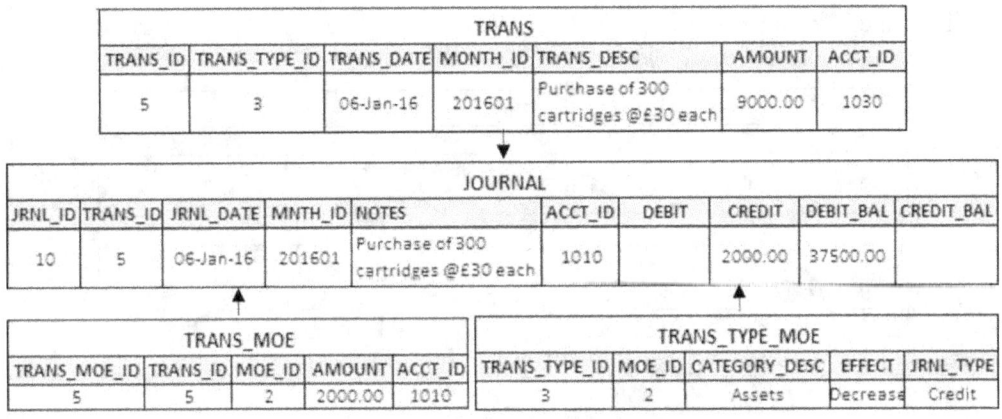

TRANS

TRANS_ID	TRANS_TYPE_ID	TRANS_DATE	MONTH_ID	TRANS_DESC	AMOUNT	ACCT_ID
5	3	06-Jan-16	201601	Purchase of 300 cartridges @£30 each	9000.00	1030

JOURNAL

JRNL_ID	TRANS_ID	JRNL_DATE	MNTH_ID	NOTES	ACCT_ID	DEBIT	CREDIT	DEBIT_BAL	CREDIT_BAL
10	5	06-Jan-16	201601	Purchase of 300 cartridges @£30 each	1010		2000.00	37500.00	

TRANS_MOE

TRANS_MOE_ID	TRANS_ID	MOE_ID	AMOUNT	ACCT_ID
5	5	2	2000.00	1010

TRANS_TYPE_MOE

TRANS_TYPE_ID	MOE_ID	CATEGORY_DESC	EFFECT	JRNL_TYPE
3	2	Assets	Decrease	Credit

Transaction 5.5.5 Bank decrease journal

- Increase in liability

The increase in liability to Toks Wholesalers is stored as

TRANS

TRANS_ID	TRANS_TYPE_ID	TRANS_DATE	MONTH_ID	TRANS_DESC	AMOUNT	ACCT_ID
5	3	06-Jan-16	201601	Purchase of 300 cartridges @£30 each	9000.00	1030

JOURNAL

JRNL_ID	TRANS_ID	JRNL_DATE	MNTH_ID	NOTES	ACCT_ID	DEBIT	CREDIT	DEBIT_BAL	CREDIT_BAL
11	5	06-Jan-16	201601	Purchase of 300 cartridges @£30 each	2001		7000.00		7000.00

TRANS_MOE

TRANS_MOE_ID	TRANS_ID	MOE_ID	AMOUNT	ACCT_ID
6	5	3	7000.00	2001

TRANS_TYPE_MOE

TRANS_TYPE_ID	MOE_ID	CATEGORY_DESC	EFFECT	JRNL_TYPE
3	3	Liabilities	Increase	Credit

Transaction 5.5.6 Liabilities increase journal

The month's summary for the bank account is updated, and summary records for the inventory and Toks Wholesalers accounts created in the ledger as follows:

LEDGER

LEDGER_ID	ACCT_ID	MNTH_ID	DEBIT	CREDIT	DEBIT_BAL	CREDIT_BAL
2	1010	201601	45000.00	7500.00	37500.00	
6	1030	201601	9000.00		9000.00	
7	2001	201601		7000.00		7000.00

Transaction 5.5.7 Bank, inventory and creditor account summaries

(f) On January 12, forty cartridges were sold for cash at £50 each.

The sale, which primarily impacts the sales revenue account, is recorded as

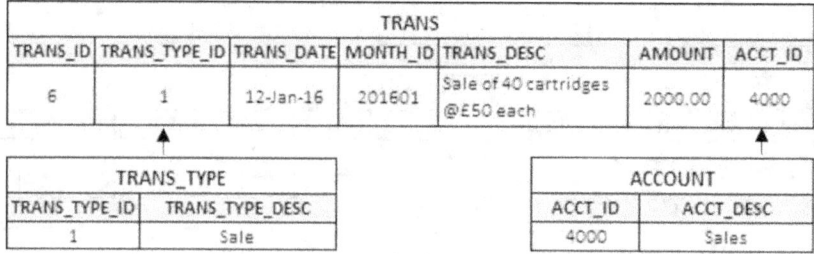

Transaction 5.6.1 Sale

The cash receipt details are stored as

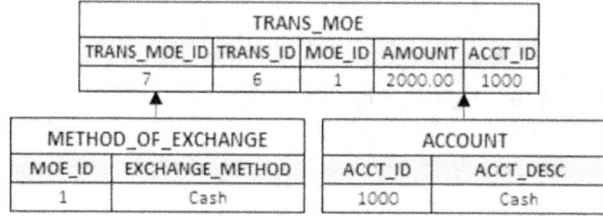

Transaction 5.6.2 Cash sale receipt

The expense of £30 incurred on each of the forty cartridges sold is recorded as

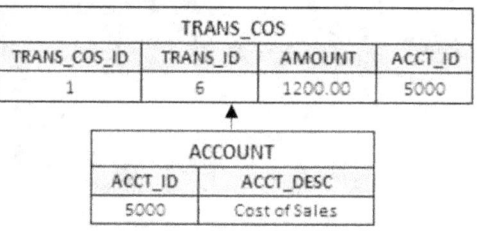

Transaction 5.6.3 Expense incurred in goods sold

The change in the value of inventory held is recorded as

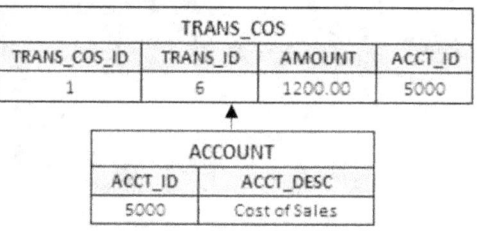

Transaction 5.6.4 Inventory reduction

The following four journal entries are generated:

- Increase in sales revenue

The increase in revenue is recorded as

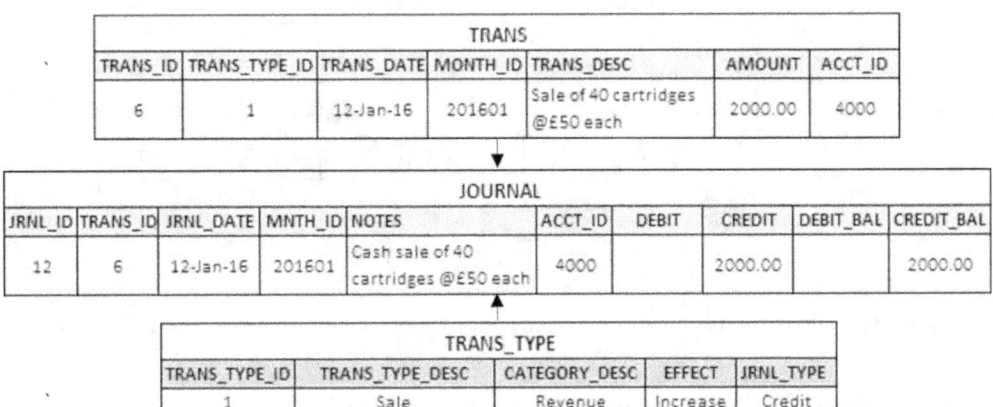

TRANS						
TRANS_ID	TRANS_TYPE_ID	TRANS_DATE	MONTH_ID	TRANS_DESC	AMOUNT	ACCT_ID
6	1	12-Jan-16	201601	Sale of 40 cartridges @£50 each	2000.00	4000

JOURNAL									
JRNL_ID	TRANS_ID	JRNL_DATE	MNTH_ID	NOTES	ACCT_ID	DEBIT	CREDIT	DEBIT_BAL	CREDIT_BAL
12	6	12-Jan-16	201601	Cash sale of 40 cartridges @£50 each	4000		2000.00		2000.00

TRANS_TYPE				
TRANS_TYPE_ID	TRANS_TYPE_DESC	CATEGORY_DESC	EFFECT	JRNL_TYPE
1	Sale	Revenue	Increase	Credit

Transaction 5.6.5 Revenue increase journal

- Increase in cash

The increase in cash is stored as

TRANS						
TRANS_ID	TRANS_TYPE_ID	TRANS_DATE	MONTH_ID	TRANS_DESC	AMOUNT	ACCT_ID
6	1	12-Jan-16	201601	Sale of 40 cartridges @£50 each	2000.00	4000

JOURNAL									
JRNL_ID	TRANS_ID	JRNL_DATE	MNTH_ID	NOTES	ACCT_ID	DEBIT	CREDIT	DEBIT_BAL	CREDIT_BAL
13	6	12-Jan-16	201601	Cash sale of 40 cartridges @£50 each	1000	2000.00		2000.00	

TRANS_MOE						TRANS_TYPE_MOE				
TRANS_MOE_ID	TRANS_ID	MOE_ID	AMOUNT	ACCT_ID		TRANS_TYPE_ID	MOE_ID	CATEGORY_DESC	EFFECT	JRNL_TYPE
7	6	1	2000.00	1000		1	1	Assets	Increase	Debit

Transaction 5.6.6 Cash increase journal

- Increase in cost of sales

The increase in the cost of sales expense is recorded as

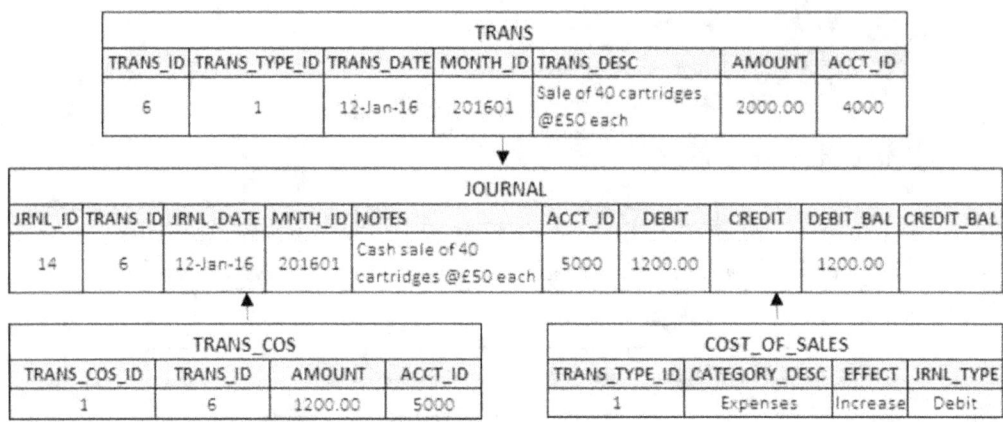

TRANS						
TRANS_ID	TRANS_TYPE_ID	TRANS_DATE	MONTH_ID	TRANS_DESC	AMOUNT	ACCT_ID
6	1	12-Jan-16	201601	Sale of 40 cartridges @£50 each	2000.00	4000

JOURNAL									
JRNL_ID	TRANS_ID	JRNL_DATE	MNTH_ID	NOTES	ACCT_ID	DEBIT	CREDIT	DEBIT_BAL	CREDIT_BAL
14	6	12-Jan-16	201601	Cash sale of 40 cartridges @£50 each	5000	1200.00		1200.00	

TRANS_COS			
TRANS_COS_ID	TRANS_ID	AMOUNT	ACCT_ID
1	6	1200.00	5000

COST_OF_SALES			
TRANS_TYPE_ID	CATEGORY_DESC	EFFECT	JRNL_TYPE
1	Expenses	Increase	Debit

Transaction 5.6.7 Cost of sales journal

- Decrease in inventory

The decrease in the inventory current asset is recorded as

TRANS						
TRANS_ID	TRANS_TYPE_ID	TRANS_DATE	MONTH_ID	TRANS_DESC	AMOUNT	ACCT_ID
6	1	12-Jan-16	201601	Sale of 40 cartridges @£50 each	2000.00	4000

JOURNAL									
JRNL_ID	TRANS_ID	JRNL_DATE	MNTH_ID	NOTES	ACCT_ID	DEBIT	CREDIT	DEBIT_BAL	CREDIT_BAL
15	6	12-Jan-16	201601	Cash sale of 40 cartridges @£50 each	1030		1200.00	7800.00	

TRANS_INV_CHANGE			
TRANS_INV_ID	TRANS_ID	AMOUNT	ACCT_ID
1	6	1200.00	1030

COS_INV_CHANGE			
TRANS_TYPE_ID	CATEGORY_DESC	EFFECT	JRNL_TYPE
1	Assets	Decrease	Credit

Transaction 5.6.8 Inventory decrease journal

The month's summary for the inventory account is updated, and summary records for cash, sales, and cost of sales accounts created in the ledger as follows:

LEDGER						
LEDGER_ID	ACCT_ID	MNTH_ID	DEBIT	CREDIT	DEBIT_BAL	CREDIT_BAL
6	1030	201601	9000.00	1200.00	7800.00	
8	1000	201601	2000.00		2000.00	
9	4000	201601		2000.00		2000.00
10	5000	201601	1200.00		1200.00	1200.00

Transaction 5.6.9 Cash, inventory, revenue and cost of sales account summaries

(g) On January 14, ten faulty cartridges were returned to Toks Wholesalers, reducing amount payable to them by £300.

The transaction is recognized as purchase returns, which primarily impacts the inventory account. It is recorded as

TRANS						
TRANS_ID	TRANS_TYPE_ID	TRANS_DATE	MONTH_ID	TRANS_DESC	AMOUNT	ACCT_ID
7	4	14-Jan-16	201601	Return of 10 faulty cartridges to supplier	300.00	1030

TRANS_TYPE	
TRANS_TYPE_ID	TRANS_TYPE_DESC
4	Purchase returns

ACCOUNT	
ACCT_ID	ACCT_DESC
1030	Inventory

Transaction 5.7.1 Purchase returns (outward)

The reduction of amount payable to the supplier is recorded in the TRANS_MOE tables as

TRANS_MOE				
TRANS_MOE_ID	TRANS_ID	MOE_ID	AMOUNT	ACCT_ID
8	7	3	300.00	2001

METHOD_OF_EXCHANGE	
MOE_ID	EXCHANGE_METHOD
3	Credit

ACCOUNT	
ACCT_ID	ACCT_DESC
2001	Toks Wholesalers

Transaction 5.7.2 Adjustment of amount payable to supplier

The following two journal entries are generated:

- Decrease in inventory

The decrease in inventory is recorded as

TRANS						
TRANS_ID	TRANS_TYPE_ID	TRANS_DATE	MONTH_ID	TRANS_DESC	AMOUNT	ACCT_ID
7	4	14-Jan-16	201601	Return of 10 faulty cartridges to supplier	300.00	1030

JOURNAL									
JRNL_ID	TRANS_ID	JRNL_DATE	MNTH_ID	NOTES	ACCT_ID	DEBIT	CREDIT	DEBIT_BAL	CREDIT_BAL
16	7	14-Jan-16	201601	Return of 10 faulty cartridges to supplier	1030		300.00	7500.00	

TRANS_TYPE				
TRANS_TYPE_ID	TRANS_TYPE_DESC	CATEGORY_DESC	EFFECT	JRNL_TYPE
4	Purchase returns	Assets	Decrease	Credit

Transaction 5.7.3 Inventory decrease journal

- Decrease in liabilities

The decrease in the amount payable to Toks Wholesalers is stored as

TRANS						
TRANS_ID	TRANS_TYPE_ID	TRANS_DATE	MONTH_ID	TRANS_DESC	AMOUNT	ACCT_ID
7	4	14-Jan-16	201601	Return of 10 faulty cartridges to supplier	300.00	1030

JOURNAL									
JRNL_ID	TRANS_ID	JRNL_DATE	MNTH_ID	NOTES	ACCT_ID	DEBIT	CREDIT	DEBIT_BAL	CREDIT_BAL
17	7	14-Jan-16	201601	Return of 10 faulty cartridges to supplier	2001	300.00			6700.00

TRANS_MOE					TRANS_TYPE_MOE				
TRANS_MOE_ID	TRANS_ID	MOE_ID	AMOUNT	ACCT_ID	TRANS_TYPE_ID	MOE_ID	CATEGORY_DESC	EFFECT	JRNL_TYPE
8	7	3	300.00	2001	4	3	Liabilities	Decrease	Debit

Transaction 5.7.4 Amount payable adjustment journal

Summary details of the inventory and Toks Wholesalers accounts are updated in the ledger as follows:

LEDGER						
LEDGER_ID	ACCT_ID	MNTH_ID	DEBIT	CREDIT	DEBIT_BAL	CREDIT_BAL
6	1030	201601	9000.00	1500.00	7500.00	
7	2001	201601	300.00	7000.00	300.00	6700.00

Transaction 5.7.5 Inventory and creditor account summaries

(h) On January 16, one hundred cartridges were sold to TeeBee Vido Limited for £55 each, who paid £500 cash, £1,500 by cheque, and agreed to settle the balance of £3,500 in thirty days.

The sale transaction, which primarily impacts sales revenue, is recorded as

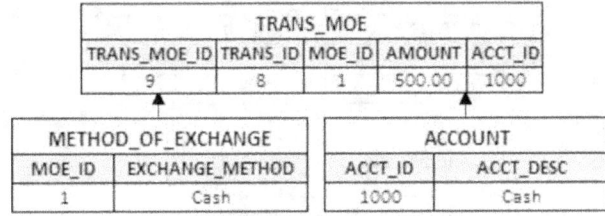

TRANS						
TRANS_ID	TRANS_TYPE_ID	TRANS_DATE	MONTH_ID	TRANS_DESC	AMOUNT	ACCT_ID
8	1	16-Jan-16	201601	Sale of 100 cartridges @ £55 each	5500.00	4000

TRANS_TYPE		ACCOUNT	
TRANS_TYPE_ID	TRANS_TYPE_DESC	ACCT_ID	ACCT_DESC
1	Sale	4000	Sales

Transaction 5.8.1 Sale

The cash payment is stored in the TRANS_MOE table as

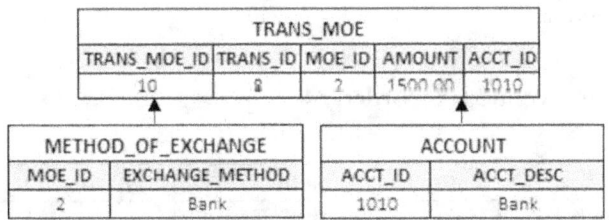

TRANS_MOE				
TRANS_MOE_ID	TRANS_ID	MOE_ID	AMOUNT	ACCT_ID
9	8	1	500.00	1000

METHOD_OF_EXCHANGE		ACCOUNT	
MOE_ID	EXCHANGE_METHOD	ACCT_ID	ACCT_DESC
1	Cash	1000	Cash

Transaction 5.8.2 Sale cash receipt

The cheque payment is stored in the TRANS_MOE table as

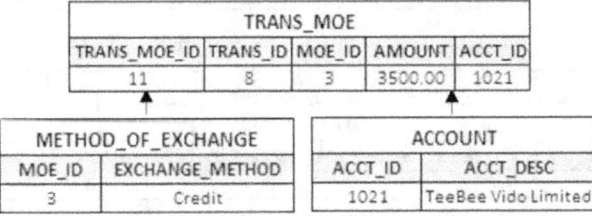

TRANS_MOE				
TRANS_MOE_ID	TRANS_ID	MOE_ID	AMOUNT	ACCT_ID
10	8	2	1500.00	1010

METHOD_OF_EXCHANGE		ACCOUNT	
MOE_ID	EXCHANGE_METHOD	ACCT_ID	ACCT_DESC
2	Bank	1010	Bank

Transaction 5.8.3 Sale cheque receipt

The amount receivable in thirty days from TeeBee Vido Limited is recorded as

TRANS_MOE				
TRANS_MOE_ID	TRANS_ID	MOE_ID	AMOUNT	ACCT_ID
11	8	3	3500.00	1021

METHOD_OF_EXCHANGE		ACCOUNT	
MOE_ID	EXCHANGE_METHOD	ACCT_ID	ACCT_DESC
3	Credit	1021	TeeBee Vido Limited

Transaction 5.8.4 Balance receivable from customer

The expense incurred of £30 on each of the one hundred cartridges sold is recorded as

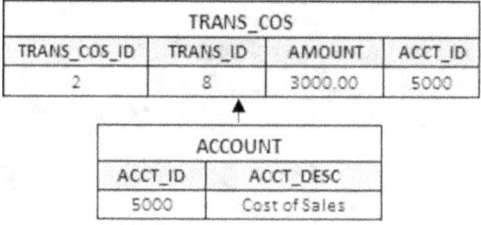

TRANS_COS			
TRANS_COS_ID	TRANS_ID	AMOUNT	ACCT_ID
2	8	3000.00	5000

ACCOUNT	
ACCT_ID	ACCT_DESC
5000	Cost of Sales

Transaction 5.8.5 Expense incurred in goods sold

The change in the value of inventory held is recorded as

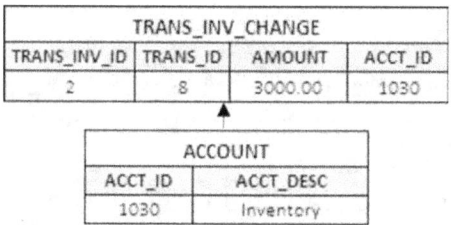

TRANS_INV_CHANGE			
TRANS_INV_ID	TRANS_ID	AMOUNT	ACCT_ID
2	8	3000.00	1030

ACCOUNT	
ACCT_ID	ACCT_DESC
1030	Inventory

Transaction 5.8.6 Inventory reduction by goods sold

The following six journal entries are generated:

- Increase in revenue

The increase in revenue is recorded as

TRANS						
TRANS_ID	TRANS_TYPE_ID	TRANS_DATE	MONTH_ID	TRANS_DESC	AMOUNT	ACCT_ID
8	1	16-Jan-16	201601	Sale of 100 cartridges @ £55 each	5500.00	4000

JOURNAL									
JRNL_ID	TRANS_ID	JRNL_DATE	MNTH_ID	NOTES	ACCT_ID	DEBIT	CREDIT	DEBIT_BAL	CREDIT_BAL
18	8	16-Jan-16	201601	Sale of 100 cartridges @ £55 each	4000		5500.00		7500.00

TRANS_TYPE				
TRANS_TYPE_ID	TRANS_TYPE_DESC	CATEGORY_DESC	EFFECT	JRNL_TYPE
1	Sale	Revenue	Increase	Credit

Transaction 5.8.7 Sale journal

- Increase in cash

The increase in cash is stored as

TRANS						
TRANS_ID	TRANS_TYPE_ID	TRANS_DATE	MONTH_ID	TRANS_DESC	AMOUNT	ACCT_ID
8	1	16-Jan-16	201601	Sale of 100 cartridges @ £55 each	5500.00	4000

JOURNAL									
JRNL_ID	TRANS_ID	JRNL_DATE	MNTH_ID	NOTES	ACCT_ID	DEBIT	CREDIT	DEBIT_BAL	CREDIT_BAL
19	8	16-Jan-16	201601	Sale of 100 cartridges @ £55 each	1000	500.00		2500.00	

TRANS_MOE						TRANS_TYPE_MOE				
TRANS_MOE_ID	TRANS_ID	MOE_ID	AMOUNT	ACCT_ID		TRANS_TYPE_ID	MOE_ID	CATEGORY_DESC	EFFECT	JRNL_TYPE
9	8	1	500.00	1000		1	1	Assets	Increase	Debit

Transaction 5.8.8 Cash increase journal

- Increase in the bank balance

The increase in the bank balance is recorded as

TRANS						
TRANS_ID	TRANS_TYPE_ID	TRANS_DATE	MONTH_ID	TRANS_DESC	AMOUNT	ACCT_ID
8	1	16-Jan-16	201601	Sale of 100 cartridges @ £55 each	5500.00	4000

JOURNAL									
JRNL_ID	TRANS_ID	JRNL_DATE	MNTH_ID	NOTES	ACCT_ID	DEBIT	CREDIT	DEBIT_BAL	CREDIT_BAL
20	8	16-Jan-16	201601	Sale of 100 cartridges @ £55 each	1010	1500.00		39000.00	

TRANS_MOE						TRANS_TYPE_MOE				
TRANS_MOE_ID	TRANS_ID	MOE_ID	AMOUNT	ACCT_ID		TRANS_TYPE_ID	MOE_ID	CATEGORY_DESC	EFFECT	JRNL_TYPE
10	8	2	1500.00	1010		1	2	Assets	Increase	Debit

Transaction 5.8.9 Bank increase journal

- Increase in amount receivable

The amount receivable from TeeBee Vido is recorded as

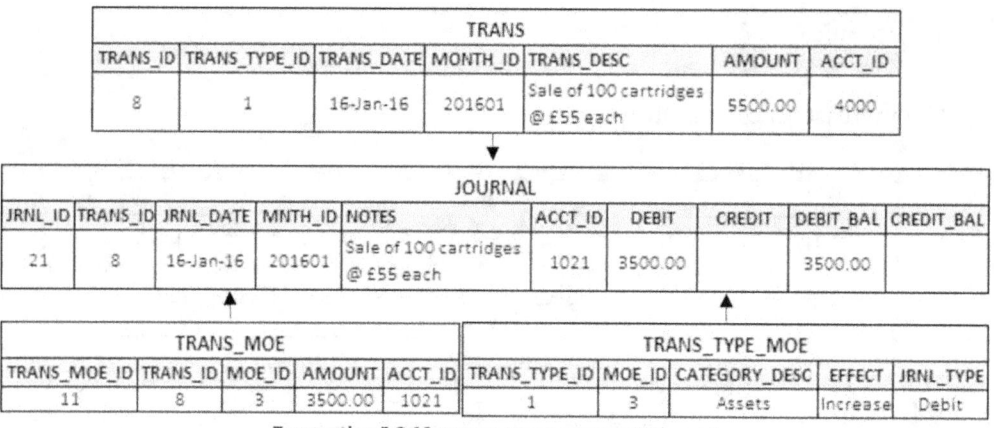

Transaction 5.8.10 Increase of amount receivable journal

- Expense of goods sold

The expense incurred in goods sold is recorded as

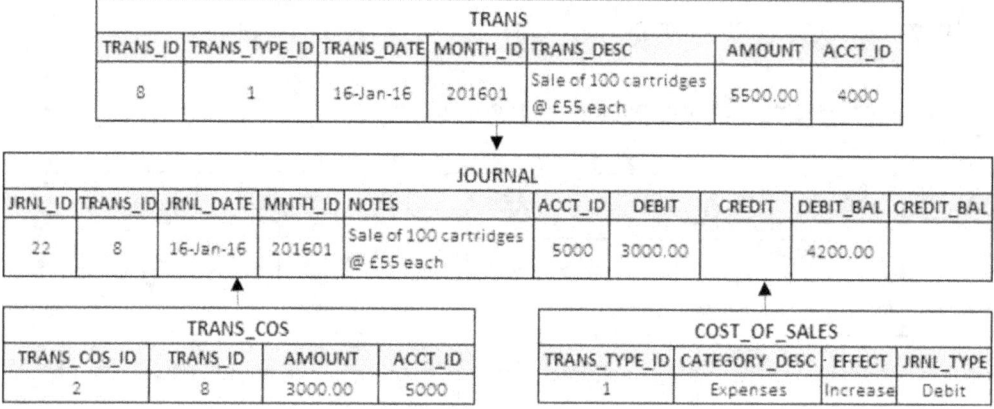

Transaction 5.8.11 Cost of sales increase journal

- Decrease in inventory

The decrease in inventory is recorded as

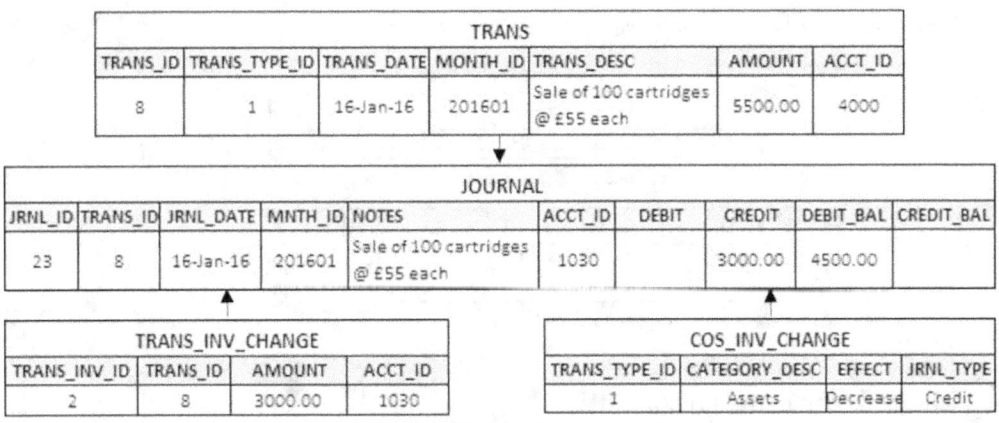

TRANS						
TRANS_ID	TRANS_TYPE_ID	TRANS_DATE	MONTH_ID	TRANS_DESC	AMOUNT	ACCT_ID
8	1	16-Jan-16	201601	Sale of 100 cartridges @ £55 each	5500.00	4000

JOURNAL									
JRNL_ID	TRANS_ID	JRNL_DATE	MNTH_ID	NOTES	ACCT_ID	DEBIT	CREDIT	DEBIT_BAL	CREDIT_BAL
23	8	16-Jan-16	201601	Sale of 100 cartridges @ £55 each	1030		3000.00	4500.00	

TRANS_INV_CHANGE			
TRANS_INV_ID	TRANS_ID	AMOUNT	ACCT_ID
2	8	3000.00	1030

COS_INV_CHANGE			
TRANS_TYPE_ID	CATEGORY_DESC	EFFECT	JRNL_TYPE
1	Assets	Decrease	Credit

Transaction 5.8.12 Inventory decrease journal

Summary details for the six accounts impacted are updated in the ledger as follows:

LEDGER						
LEDGER_ID	ACCT_ID	MNTH_ID	DEBIT	CREDIT	DEBIT_BAL	CREDIT_BAL
2	1010	201601	46500.00	7500.00	39000.00	
6	1030	201601	9000.00	4500.00	4500.00	
8	1000	201601	2500.00		2500.00	
9	4000	201601		7500.00		7500.00
10	5000	201601	4200.00		4200.00	
11	1021	201601	3500.00		3500.00	

Transaction 5.8.13 Summaries of accounts impacted

(i) On January 19, three laptops for use in the business were bought for £784 each, and a payment of £1,352 by cheque and £1,000 in cash was made.

The transaction, regarded as a purchase of a noncurrent asset, primarily impacting the computer hardware account, is recorded as

TRANS						
TRANS_ID	TRANS_TYPE_ID	TRANS_DATE	MONTH_ID	TRANS_DESC	AMOUNT	ACCT_ID
9	8	19-Jan-16	201601	Purchase of 3 laptops for use for £784 each	2352.00	1500

TRANS_TYPE	
TRANS_TYPE_ID	TRANS_TYPE_DESC
8	Purchase of non-current asset

ACCOUNT	
ACCT_ID	ACCT_DESC
1500	Computer Hardware

Transaction 5.9.1 Purchase of non-current assets

The payment by cheque is recorded as

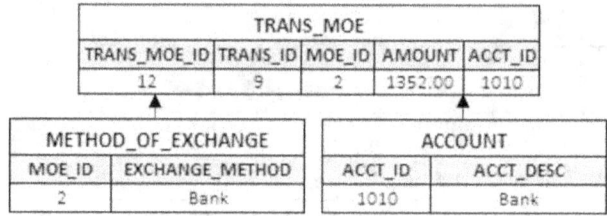

TRANS_MOE				
TRANS_MOE_ID	TRANS_ID	MOE_ID	AMOUNT	ACCT_ID
12	9	2	1352.00	1010

METHOD_OF_EXCHANGE	
MOE_ID	EXCHANGE_METHOD
2	Bank

ACCOUNT	
ACCT_ID	ACCT_DESC
1010	Bank

Transaction 5.9.2 Cheque payment to supplier

The cash payment is recorded as

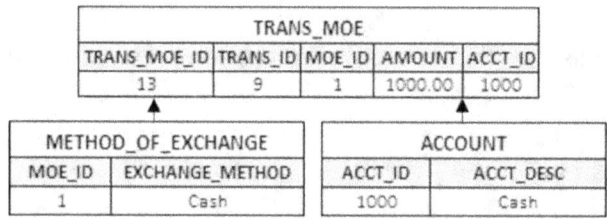

TRANS_MOE				
TRANS_MOE_ID	TRANS_ID	MOE_ID	AMOUNT	ACCT_ID
13	9	1	1000.00	1000

METHOD_OF_EXCHANGE	
MOE_ID	EXCHANGE_METHOD
1	Cash

ACCOUNT	
ACCT_ID	ACCT_DESC
1000	Cash

Transaction 5.9.3 Cash payment to supplier

The following three journal entries are generated:

- Increase in computer hardware

Journal entry details to record increase in the computer hardware account are stored as

TRANS						
TRANS_ID	TRANS_TYPE_ID	TRANS_DATE	MONTH_ID	TRANS_DESC	AMOUNT	ACCT_ID
9	8	19-Jan-16	201601	Purchase of 3 laptops for use for £784 each	2352.00	1500

JOURNAL									
JRNL_ID	TRANS_ID	JRNL_DATE	MNTH_ID	NOTES	ACCT_ID	DEBIT	CREDIT	DEBIT_BAL	CREDIT_BAL
24	9	19-Jan-16	201601	Purchase of 3 laptops for use for £784 each	1500	2352.00		2352.00	

TRANS_TYPE				
TRANS_TYPE_ID	TRANS_TYPE_DESC	CATEGORY_DESC	EFFECT	JRNL_TYPE
8	Purchase of non-current asset	Assets	Increase	Debit

Transaction 5.9.4 Computer hardware increase journal

- Decrease in bank account

The journal entry that records a decrease in the balance of the bank account is stored as

TRANS						
TRANS_ID	TRANS_TYPE_ID	TRANS_DATE	MONTH_ID	TRANS_DESC	AMOUNT	ACCT_ID
9	8	19-Jan-16	201601	Purchase of 3 laptops for use for £784 each	2352.00	1500

JOURNAL									
JRNL_ID	TRANS_ID	JRNL_DATE	MNTH_ID	NOTES	ACCT_ID	DEBIT	CREDIT	DEBIT_BAL	CREDIT_BAL
25	9	19-Jan-16	201601	Purchase of 3 laptops for use for £784 each	1010		1352.00	37648.00	

TRANS_MOE						TRANS_TYPE_MOE				
TRANS_MOE_ID	TRANS_ID	MOE_ID	AMOUNT	ACCT_ID		TRANS_TYPE_ID	MOE_ID	CATEGORY_DESC	EFFECT	JRNL_TYPE
12	9	2	1352.00	1010		8	2	Assets	Decrease	Credit

Transaction 5.9.5 Bank decrease journal

- Decrease in cash

The decrease in cash is recorded as

TRANS						
TRANS_ID	TRANS_TYPE_ID	TRANS_DATE	MONTH_ID	TRANS_DESC	AMOUNT	ACCT_ID
9	8	19-Jan-16	201601	Purchase of 3 laptops for use for £784 each	2352.00	1500

JOURNAL									
JRNL_ID	TRANS_ID	JRNL_DATE	MNTH_ID	NOTES	ACCT_ID	DEBIT	CREDIT	DEBIT_BAL	CREDIT_BAL
26	9	19-Jan-16	201601	Purchase of 3 laptops for use for £784 each	1000		1000.00	1500.00	

TRANS_MOE						TRANS_TYPE_MOE				
TRANS_MOE_ID	TRANS_ID	MOE_ID	AMOUNT	ACCT_ID		TRANS_TYPE_ID	MOE_ID	CATEGORY_DESC	EFFECT	JRNL_TYPE
13	9	1	1000.00	1000		8	1	Assets	Decrease	Credit

Transaction 5.9.6 Cash decrease journal

The month's summary details of the accounts affected are updated as follows:

LEDGER						
LEDGER_ID	ACCT_ID	MNTH_ID	DEBIT	CREDIT	DEBIT_BAL	CREDIT_BAL
2	1010	201601	46500.00	8852.00	37648.00	
8	1000	201601	2500.00	1000.00	1500.00	
12	1500	201601	2352.00		2352.00	

Transaction 5.9.7 Cash, bank and computer hardware account summaries

(j) On January 21, TeeBee Vido Limited returned twenty cartridges excess to requirements, reducing the amount receivable from them by £1,100.

The sales returns transaction, which primarily impacts the sales returns account, is recorded as

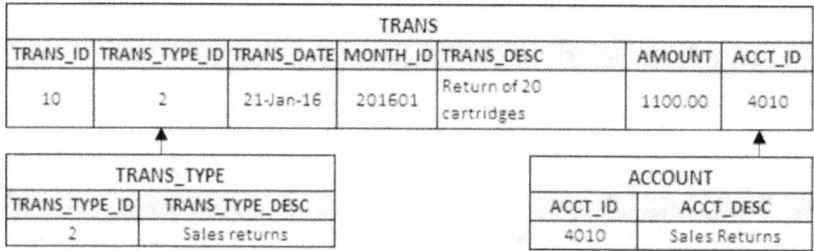

Transaction 5.10.1 Sales returns (inwards)

The decrease in amount receivable from TeeBee Vido Limited is recorded in the TRANS_MOE table as

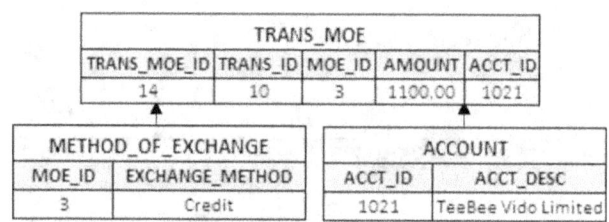

Transaction 5.10.2 Adjustment of amount receivable from customer

The recovery of the expense of £600 incurred on the twenty cartridges returned is recorded as

TRANS_COS			
TRANS_COS_ID	TRANS_ID	AMOUNT	ACCT_ID
3	10	600.00	5000

ACCOUNT	
ACCT_ID	ACCT_DESC
5000	Cost of Sales

Transaction 5.10.3 Goods sold expense recovery

The change in the value of inventory held is recorded as

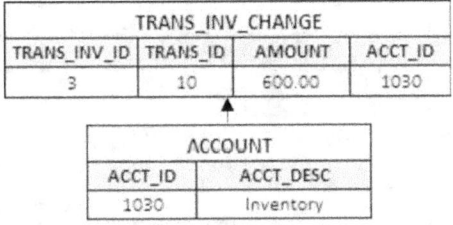

TRANS_INV_CHANGE			
TRANS_INV_ID	TRANS_ID	AMOUNT	ACCT_ID
3	10	600.00	1030

ACCOUNT	
ACCT_ID	ACCT_DESC
1030	Inventory

Transaction 5.10.4 Inventory increase

The following four journal entries are generated:

- Decrease in revenue

The decrease in revenue is recorded as

TRANS						
TRANS_ID	TRANS_TYPE_ID	TRANS_DATE	MONTH_ID	TRANS_DESC	AMOUNT	ACCT_ID
10	2	21-Jan-16	201601	Return of 20 cartridges	1100.00	4010

JOURNAL									
JRNL_ID	TRANS_ID	JRNL_DATE	MNTH_ID	NOTES	ACCT_ID	DEBIT	CREDIT	DEBIT_BAL	CREDIT_BAL
27	10	21-Jan-16	201601	Return of 20 cartridges	4010	1100.00		1100.00	

TRANS_TYPE				
TRANS_TYPE_ID	TRANS_TYPE_DESC	CATEGORY_DESC	EFFECT	JRNL_TYPE
2	Sales returns	Revenue	Decrease	Debit

Transaction 5.10.5 Revenue decrease journal

- Decrease in amount receivable

The decrease in amount receivable from TeeBee Vido Limited is stored as

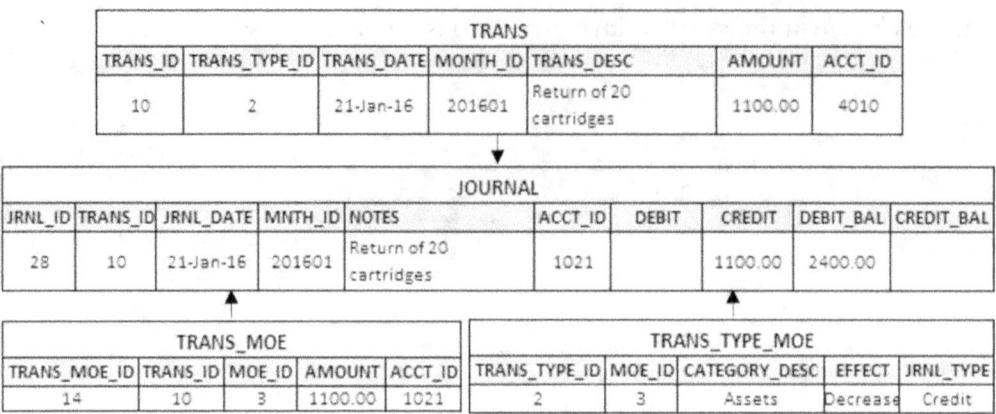

Transaction 5.10.6 Amount receivable decrease journal

- Decrease in cost of sales

  The decrease in cost of sales expense is recorded as

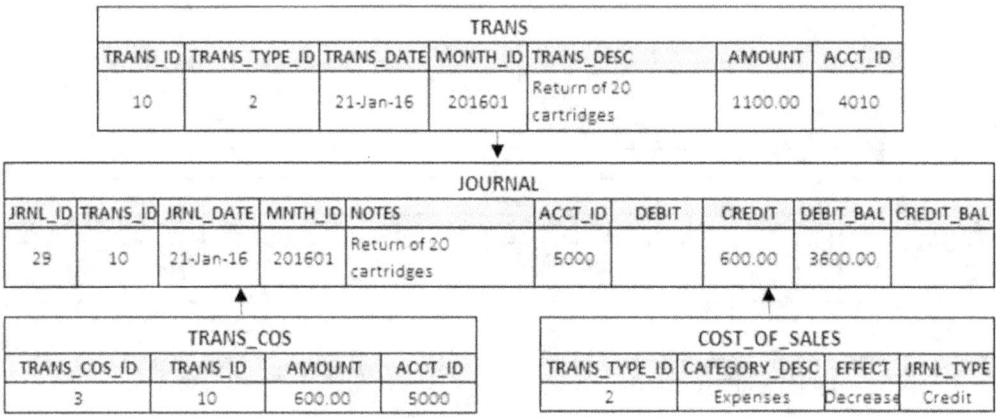

Transaction 5.10.7 Cost of sales decrease journal

- Increase in inventory

  The increase in inventory is recorded as

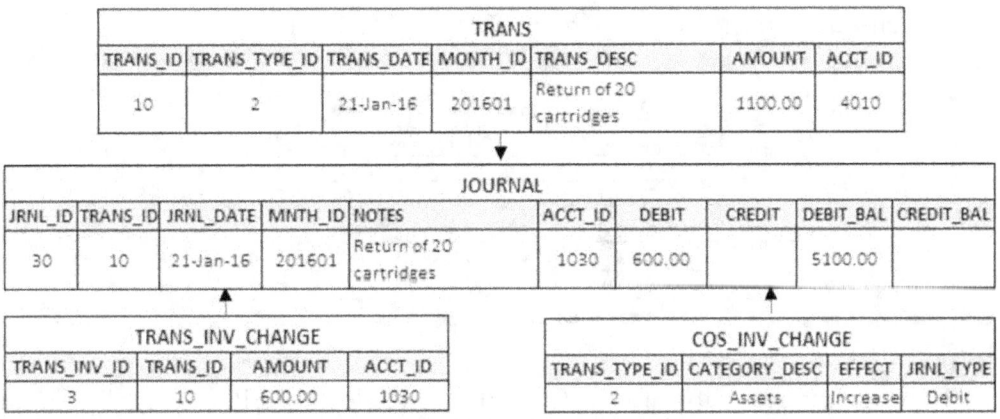

Transaction 5.10.8 Inventry increase journal

Summary details of the four accounts impacted are updated in the ledger as follows:

LEDGER						
LEDGER_ID	ACCT_ID	MNTH_ID	DEBIT	CREDIT	DEBIT_BAL	CREDIT_BAL
6	1030	201601	9600.00	4500.00	5100.00	
10	5000	201601	4200.00	600.00	3600.00	
11	1021	201601	3500.00	1100.00	2400.00	
13	4010	201601	1100.00		1100.00	

Transaction 5.10.9 Sales returns, customer, inventory and cost of sales summaries

(k) On January 23, 120 cartridges were sold to Tailspin & Mandown LLP for £55 each, received a cheque of £2,000, and the difference receivable in thirty days.

The sales transaction, which primarily impacts sales revenue, is recorded as

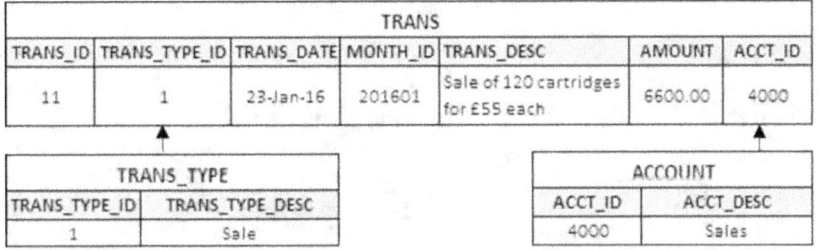

Transaction 5.11.1 Sale

The cheque payment is stored in the TRANS_MOE table as:

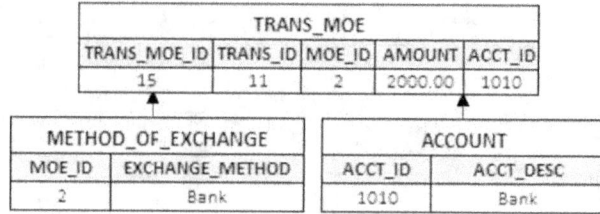

TRANS_MOE

TRANS_MOE_ID	TRANS_ID	MOE_ID	AMOUNT	ACCT_ID
15	11	2	2000.00	1010

METHOD_OF_EXCHANGE

MOE_ID	EXCHANGE_METHOD
2	Bank

ACCOUNT

ACCT_ID	ACCT_DESC
1010	Bank

Transaction 5.11.2 Sale cheque receipt

The amount receivable from Tailspin & Mandown LLP is recorded in the TRANS_MOE table as

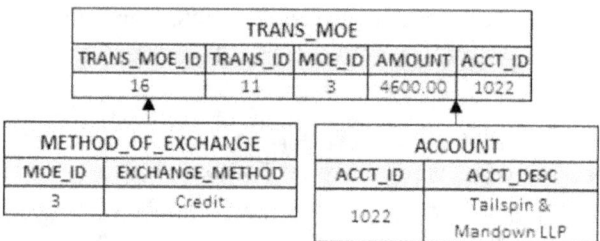

TRANS_MOE

TRANS_MOE_ID	TRANS_ID	MOE_ID	AMOUNT	ACCT_ID
16	11	3	4600.00	1022

METHOD_OF_EXCHANGE

MOE_ID	EXCHANGE_METHOD
3	Credit

ACCOUNT

ACCT_ID	ACCT_DESC
1022	Tailspin & Mandown LLP

Transaction 5.11.3 Amount receivable from customer

The expense incurred in the cartridges sold is recorded as

TRANS_COS

TRANS_COS_ID	TRANS_ID	AMOUNT	ACCT_ID
4	11	3600.00	5000

ACCOUNT

ACCT_ID	ACCT_DESC
5000	Cost of Sales

Transaction 5.11.4 Expense incurred in goods sold

The change in the value of inventory held is recorded as

TRANS_INV_CHANGE

TRANS_INV_ID	TRANS_ID	AMOUNT	ACCT_ID
4	11	3600.00	1030

ACCOUNT

ACCT_ID	ACCT_DESC
1030	Inventory

Transaction 5.11.5 Inventory decrease

The following five journal entries are generated:

- Increase in revenue

The increase in revenue is recorded as

TRANS						
TRANS_ID	TRANS_TYPE_ID	TRANS_DATE	MONTH_ID	TRANS_DESC	AMOUNT	ACCT_ID
11	1	23-Jan-16	201601	Sale of 120 cartridges for £55 each	6600.00	4000

JOURNAL									
JRNL_ID	TRANS_ID	JRNL_DATE	MNTH_ID	NOTES	ACCT_ID	DEBIT	CREDIT	DEBIT_BAL	CREDIT_BAL
31	11	23-Jan-16	201601	Sale of 120 cartridges for £55 each	4000		6600.00		14100.00

TRANS_TYPE				
TRANS_TYPE_ID	TRANS_TYPE_DESC	CATEGORY_DESC	EFFECT	JRNL_TYPE
1	Sale	Revenue	Increase	Credit

Transaction 5.11.6 Revenue increase journal

- Increase in the bank balance

Increase in the bank balance is recorded as

TRANS						
TRANS_ID	TRANS_TYPE_ID	TRANS_DATE	MONTH_ID	TRANS_DESC	AMOUNT	ACCT_ID
11	1	23-Jan-16	201601	Sale of 120 cartridges for £55 each	6600.00	4000

JOURNAL									
JRNL_ID	TRANS_ID	JRNL_DATE	MNTH_ID	NOTES	ACCT_ID	DEBIT	CREDIT	DEBIT_BAL	CREDIT_BAL
32	11	23-Jan-16	201601	Sale of 120 cartridges for £55 each	1010	2000.00		39648.00	

TRANS_MOE						TRANS_TYPE_MOE				
TRANS_MOE_ID	TRANS_ID	MOE_ID	AMOUNT	ACCT_ID		TRANS_TYPE_ID	MOE_ID	CATEGORY_DESC	EFFECT	JRNL_TYPE
15	11	2	2000.00	1010		1	2	Assets	Increase	Debit

Transaction 5.11.7 Bank increase journal

- Increase in amount receivable

The amount receivable from Tailspin & Mandown LLP is recorded as

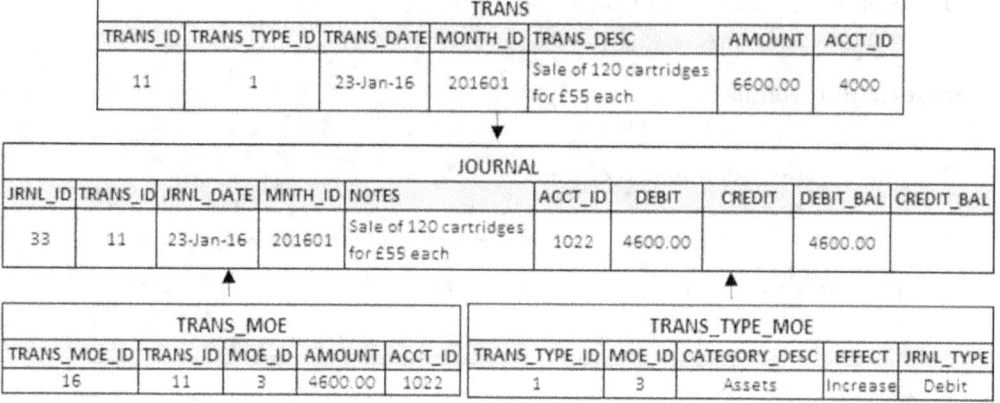

TRANS						
TRANS_ID	TRANS_TYPE_ID	TRANS_DATE	MONTH_ID	TRANS_DESC	AMOUNT	ACCT_ID
11	1	23-Jan-16	201601	Sale of 120 cartridges for £55 each	6600.00	4000

JOURNAL									
JRNL_ID	TRANS_ID	JRNL_DATE	MNTH_ID	NOTES	ACCT_ID	DEBIT	CREDIT	DEBIT_BAL	CREDIT_BAL
33	11	23-Jan-16	201601	Sale of 120 cartridges for £55 each	1022	4600.00		4600.00	

TRANS_MOE				
TRANS_MOE_ID	TRANS_ID	MOE_ID	AMOUNT	ACCT_ID
16	11	3	4600.00	1022

TRANS_TYPE_MOE				
TRANS_TYPE_ID	MOE_ID	CATEGORY_DESC	EFFECT	JRNL_TYPE
1	3	Assets	Increase	Debit

Transaction 5.11.8 Amount receivable increase journal

- Increase in cost of goods sold

   The cost incurred in buying goods sold is recorded as

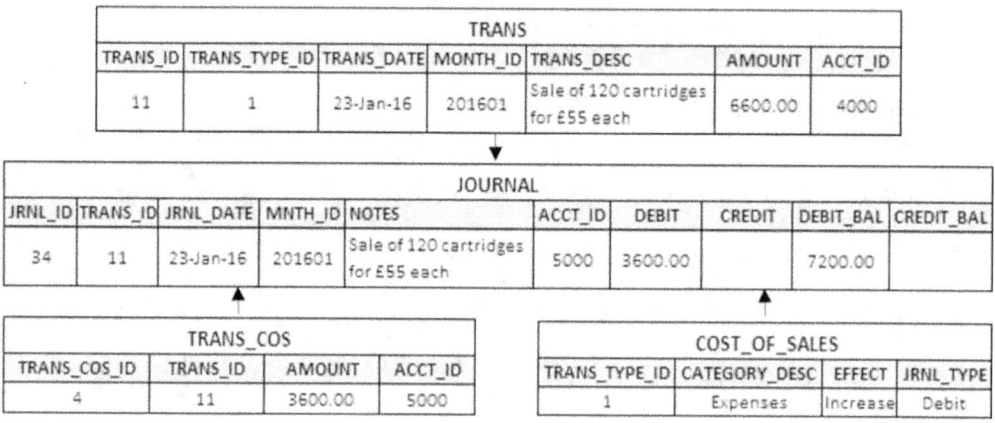

TRANS						
TRANS_ID	TRANS_TYPE_ID	TRANS_DATE	MONTH_ID	TRANS_DESC	AMOUNT	ACCT_ID
11	1	23-Jan-16	201601	Sale of 120 cartridges for £55 each	6600.00	4000

JOURNAL									
JRNL_ID	TRANS_ID	JRNL_DATE	MNTH_ID	NOTES	ACCT_ID	DEBIT	CREDIT	DEBIT_BAL	CREDIT_BAL
34	11	23-Jan-16	201601	Sale of 120 cartridges for £55 each	5000	3600.00		7200.00	

TRANS_COS			
TRANS_COS_ID	TRANS_ID	AMOUNT	ACCT_ID
4	11	3600.00	5000

COST_OF_SALES			
TRANS_TYPE_ID	CATEGORY_DESC	EFFECT	JRNL_TYPE
1	Expenses	Increase	Debit

Transaction 5.11.9 Cost of goods sold increase journal

- Decrease in inventory

   The decrease in inventory is recorded as

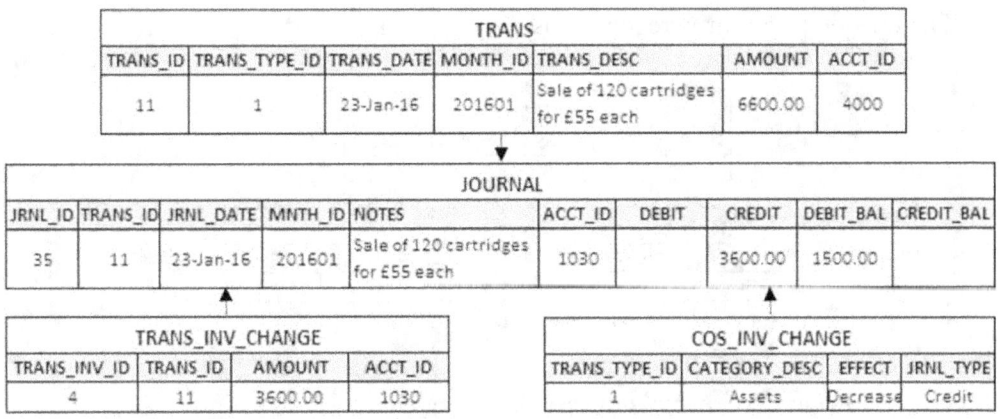

TRANS						
TRANS_ID	TRANS_TYPE_ID	TRANS_DATE	MONTH_ID	TRANS_DESC	AMOUNT	ACCT_ID
11	1	23-Jan-16	201601	Sale of 120 cartridges for £55 each	6600.00	4000

JOURNAL									
JRNL_ID	TRANS_ID	JRNL_DATE	MNTH_ID	NOTES	ACCT_ID	DEBIT	CREDIT	DEBIT_BAL	CREDIT_BAL
35	11	23-Jan-16	201601	Sale of 120 cartridges for £55 each	1030		3600.00	1500.00	

TRANS_INV_CHANGE			
TRANS_INV_ID	TRANS_ID	AMOUNT	ACCT_ID
4	11	3600.00	1030

COS_INV_CHANGE			
TRANS_TYPE_ID	CATEGORY_DESC	EFFECT	JRNL_TYPE
1	Assets	Decrease	Credit

Transaction 5.11.10 Inventory decrease journal

Summary details of the five accounts impacted are updated in the ledger as follows:

LEDGER						
LEDGER_ID	ACCT_ID	MNTH_ID	DEBIT	CREDIT	DEBIT_BAL	CREDIT_BAL
2	1010	201601	48500.00	8852.00	39648.00	
6	1030	201601	9600.00	8100.00	1500.00	
9	4000	201601		14100.00		14100.00
10	5000	201601	7800.00	600.00	7200.00	
14	1022	201601	4600.00		4600.00	

Transaction 5.11.11 Summaries of accounts impacted

(l)   On January 23, £265 was paid by cheque for telephones and internet service.

The expense transaction which primarily impacts the telephone & internet account is recorded as:

TRANS						
TRANS_ID	TRANS_TYPE_ID	TRANS_DATE	MONTH_ID	TRANS_DESC	AMOUNT	ACCT_ID
12	7	23-Jan-16	201601	Jan '16 telephone and internet service	265.00	5210

TRANS_TYPE	
TRANS_TYPE_ID	TRANS_TYPE_DESC
7	Expense

ACCOUNT	
ACCT_ID	ACCT_DESC
5210	Telephone & Internet

Transaction 5.12.1 Telehone and internet expenses

The cheque payment is recorded as:

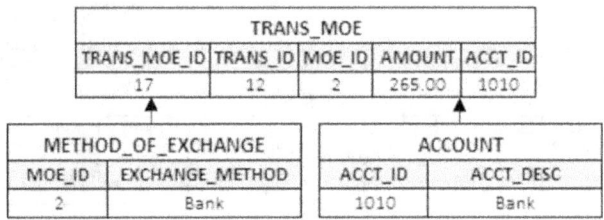

TRANS_MOE				
TRANS_MOE_ID	TRANS_ID	MOE_ID	AMOUNT	ACCT_ID
17	12	2	265.00	1010

METHOD_OF_EXCHANGE	
MOE_ID	EXCHANGE_METHOD
2	Bank

ACCOUNT	
ACCT_ID	ACCT_DESC
1010	Bank

Transaction 5.12.2 Cheque payment

The following two journal entries are generated:

- Increase in telephone and internet expense

Journal entry details to record increase in the telephone & internet expense account are stored as:

TRANS						
TRANS_ID	TRANS_TYPE_ID	TRANS_DATE	MONTH_ID	TRANS_DESC	AMOUNT	ACCT_ID
12	7	23-Jan-16	201601	Jan '16 telephone and internet service	265.00	5210

JOURNAL									
JRNL_ID	TRANS_ID	JRNL_DATE	MNTH_ID	NOTES	ACCT_ID	DEBIT	CREDIT	DEBIT_BAL	CREDIT_BAL
36	12	23-Jan-16	201601	Jan '16 telephone and internet service	5210	265.00		265.00	

TRANS_TYPE				
TRANS_TYPE_ID	TRANS_TYPE_DESC	CATEGORY_DESC	EFFECT	JRNL_TYPE
7	Expense	Expenses	Increase	Debit

Transaction 5.12.3 Expense increase journal

- Decrease in bank account

The corresponding decrease in the balance of the bank account is stored as:

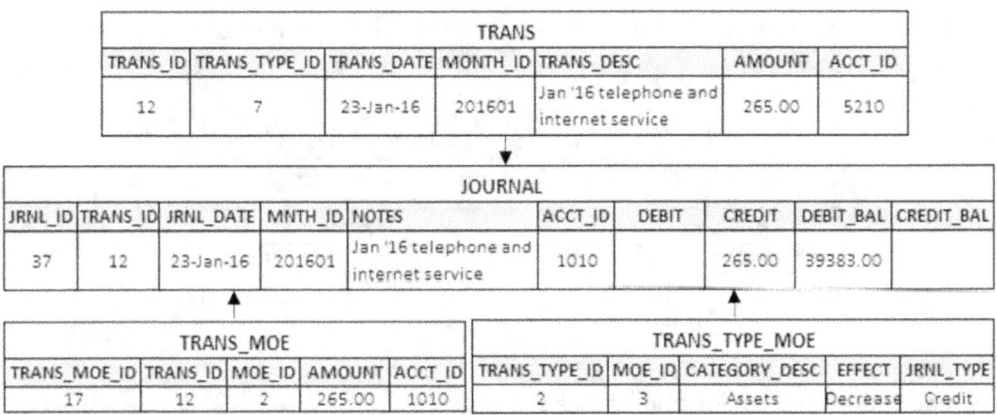

TRANS						
TRANS_ID	TRANS_TYPE_ID	TRANS_DATE	MONTH_ID	TRANS_DESC	AMOUNT	ACCT_ID
12	7	23-Jan-16	201601	Jan '16 telephone and internet service	265.00	5210

JOURNAL									
JRNL_ID	TRANS_ID	JRNL_DATE	MNTH_ID	NOTES	ACCT_ID	DEBIT	CREDIT	DEBIT_BAL	CREDIT_BAL
37	12	23-Jan-16	201601	Jan '16 telephone and internet service	1010		265.00	39383.00	

TRANS_MOE				
TRANS_MOE_ID	TRANS_ID	MOE_ID	AMOUNT	ACCT_ID
17	12	2	265.00	1010

TRANS_TYPE_MOE				
TRANS_TYPE_ID	MOE_ID	CATEGORY_DESC	EFFECT	JRNL_TYPE
2	3	Assets	Decrease	Credit

Transaction 5.12.4 Bank decrease journal

The month's summary for the bank account is updated and a summary record for telephone and internet account created in the ledger as:

LEDGER						
LEDGER_ID	ACCT_ID	MNTH_ID	DEBIT	CREDIT	DEBIT_BAL	CREDIT_BAL
2	1010	201601	48500.00	9117.00	39383.00	
15	5210	201601	265.00		265.00	

Transaction 5.12.5 Bank and telephone & internet account summaries

(m) On the 30th January, a total of £4 300 was paid out in staff salaries from the bank account.

The expense transaction which primarily impacts the salaries account is recorded as:

TRANS						
TRANS_ID	TRANS_TYPE_ID	TRANS_DATE	MONTH_ID	TRANS_DESC	AMOUNT	ACCT_ID
13	7	30-Jan-16	201601	Jan '16 Staff salaries	4300.00	5200

TRANS_TYPE	
TRANS_TYPE_ID	TRANS_TYPE_DESC
7	Expense

ACCOUNT	
ACCT_ID	ACCT_DESC
5200	Salaries

Transaction 5.13.1 Staff salaries

The total paid out from the bank account for salaries is recorded as:

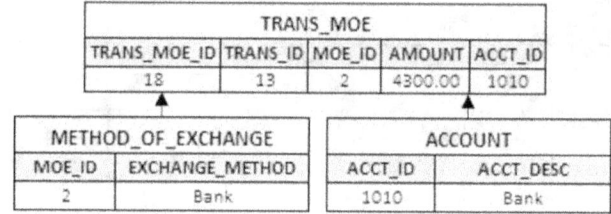

TRANS_MOE				
TRANS_MOE_ID	TRANS_ID	MOE_ID	AMOUNT	ACCT_ID
18	13	2	4300.00	1010

METHOD_OF_EXCHANGE	
MOE_ID	EXCHANGE_METHOD
2	Bank

ACCOUNT	
ACCT_ID	ACCT_DESC
1010	Bank

Transaction 5.13.2 Gross salary paid through the bank

The following two journal entries are generated:

- Increase in salaries expense

Journal entry details to record increase in the salaries expense account are stored as:

TRANS						
TRANS_ID	TRANS_TYPE_ID	TRANS_DATE	MONTH_ID	TRANS_DESC	AMOUNT	ACCT_ID
13	7	30-Jan-16	201601	Jan '16 Staff salaries	4300.00	5200

JOURNAL									
JRNL_ID	TRANS_ID	JRNL_DATE	MNTH_ID	NOTES	ACCT_ID	DEBIT	CREDIT	DEBIT_BAL	CREDIT_BAL
38	13	30-Jan-16	201601	Jan '16 Staff salaries	5200	4300.00		4300.00	

TRANS_TYPE				
TRANS_TYPE_ID	TRANS_TYPE_DESC	CATEGORY_DESC	EFFECT	JRNL_TYPE
7	Expense	Expenses	Increase	Debit

Transaction 5.13.3 Expense increase journal

- Decrease in bank account

The corresponding decrease in the balance of the bank account is stored as:

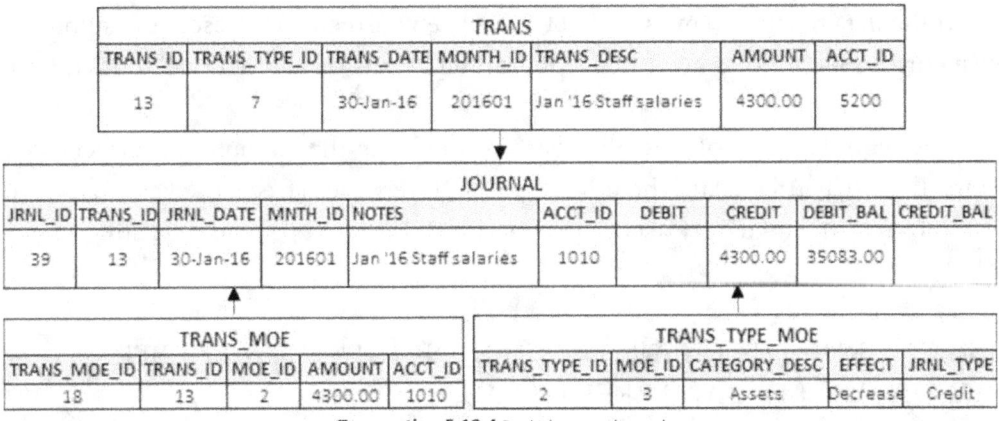

TRANS						
TRANS_ID	TRANS_TYPE_ID	TRANS_DATE	MONTH_ID	TRANS_DESC	AMOUNT	ACCT_ID
13	7	30-Jan-16	201601	Jan '16 Staff salaries	4300.00	5200

JOURNAL									
JRNL_ID	TRANS_ID	JRNL_DATE	MNTH_ID	NOTES	ACCT_ID	DEBIT	CREDIT	DEBIT_BAL	CREDIT_BAL
39	13	30-Jan-16	201601	Jan '16 Staff salaries	1010		4300.00	35083.00	

TRANS_MOE						TRANS_TYPE_MOE				
TRANS_MOE_ID	TRANS_ID	MOE_ID	AMOUNT	ACCT_ID		TRANS_TYPE_ID	MOE_ID	CATEGORY_DESC	EFFECT	JRNL_TYPE
18	13	2	4300.00	1010		2	3	Assets	Decrease	Credit

Transaction 5.13.4 Bank decrease journal

The month's summary for the bank account is updated and a summary record for salaries account created in the ledger as:

LEDGER						
LEDGER_ID	ACCT_ID	MNTH_ID	DEBIT	CREDIT	DEBIT_BAL	CREDIT_BAL
2	1010	201601	48500.00	13417.00	35083.00	
16	5200	201601	4300.00		4300.00	

Transaction 5.13.5 Bank and salaries account summaries

Summary of data collected

Transactions processed in the first month of operation has impacted 16 accounts whose summaries in the ledger are shown in Table 5.1.

LEDGER_ID	MNTH_ID	ACCT_ID	DEBIT	CREDIT	DEBIT_BAL	CREDIT_BAL
1	201601	3000	0.00	15000.00	0.00	15000.00
2	201601	1010	48500.00	13417.00	35083.00	0.00
3	201601	2500	0.00	30000.00	0.00	30000.00
4	201601	5260	1000.00	0.00	1000.00	0.00
5	201601	1520	4500.00	0.00	4500.00	0.00
6	201601	1030	9600.00	8100.00	1500.00	0.00
7	201601	2001	300.00	7000.00	0.00	6700.00
8	201601	1000	2500.00	1000.00	1500.00	0.00
9	201601	4000	0.00	14100.00	0.00	14100.00
10	201601	5000	7800.00	600.00	7200.00	0.00
11	201601	1021	3500.00	1100.00	2400.00	0.00
12	201601	1500	2352.00	0.00	2352.00	0.00
13	201601	4010	1100.00	0.00	1100.00	0.00
14	201601	1022	4600.00	0.00	4600.00	0.00
15	201601	5210	265.00	0.00	265.00	0.00
16	201601	5200	4300.00	0.00	4300.00	0.00

Table 5.1 Ledger account summaries at the end of month 201601

If the data relating to month 201601 has been correctly processed, the summaries must correspond to journal entries representing effects of transactions in the month.

The end balance of each account should be the cumulative effect of all transactions that affected it. The following TSQL retrieves effects of every transaction that impacted the inventory account in month 201601 to produce the listing in table 5.2

```
SELECT J.JRNL_DATE, P.TRANS_TYPE_DESC, J.NOTES, J.DEBIT,
J.CREDIT, J.DEBIT_BAL, J.CREDIT_BAL
FROM JOURNAL AS J
INNER JOIN TRANS AS T ON J.TRANS_ID = T.TRANS_ID
INNER JOIN TRANS_TYPE AS P ON T.TRANS_TYPE_ID =
P.TRANS_TYPE_ID
WHERE J.ACCT_ID = 1030 AND
        J.MNTH_ID = 201601
```

JRNL_DATE	TRANS_TYPE_DESC	NOTES	DEBIT	CREDIT	DEBIT_BAL	CREDIT_BAL
06-Jan-16	Purchase of goods	Purchase of 300 cartridges @£30 each	9000.00	0.00	9000.00	0.00
12-Jan-16	Sale	Sale of 40 cartridges @£50 each	0.00	1200.00	7800.00	0.00
14-Jan-16	Purchase returns	Return of 10 faulty cartridges to supplier	0.00	300.00	7500.00	0.00
16-Jan-16	Sale	Sale of 100 cartridges @ £55 each	0.00	3000.00	4500.00	0.00
21-Jan-16	Sale Returns	Return of 20 cartridges	600.00	0.00	5100.00	0.00
23-Jan-16	Sale	Sale of 120 cartridges for £55 each	0.00	3600.00	1500.00	0.00

Table 5.2 Effect of transactions on the inventory account

Once validity of the data is verified, it can be the basis of preparation of information the business can use to make informed decisions.

Chapter 6 - Data verification

Data Quality

The *adage garbage in, garbage out* underlines the significance of data quality. The consequences of wrong or incomplete accounting data are at best an inconvenience that hinders informed decision making. In some situations, inaccurate financial reporting can damage the credibility of a business.

The quality of accounting data held must be verified before it is used. At the very minimum, the data must pass the following quality tests:

- **Accuracy and completeness**

The journal and the ledger must be an accurate reflection of effects of all transactions. The data must be traceable from summary records in the ledger to source transactions.

Validation starts at transaction data entry by ensuring sufficient information is collected to create journal entries or to rebuild the journal table in the event of data corruption or data loss.

Every journal entry must have a reference to the source transaction, and the amount debited for each transaction must correspond to the amount credited. Running balances in the journal must be in sync with the month's aggregates in the ledger.

The following TSQL code, which ensures every transaction has journal entries, only returns a result set when there is a discrepancy.

```
SELECT T.TRANS_ID
FROM TRANS AS T
LEFT JOIN JOURNAL AS J ON T.TRANS_ID = J.TRANS_ID
WHERE J.TRANS_ID IS NULL
```

And the following TSQL code lists every transaction whose debits do not correspond to credits:

```
SELECT T.TRANS_ID
FROM TRANS AS T
JOIN JOURNAL AS J ON T.TRANS_ID = J.TRANS_ID
GROUP BY T.TRANS_ID
HAVING SUM(J.DEBIT) <> SUM(CREDIT)
```

The following TSQL code verifies running balances in the journal against summaries in the ledger.

```
WITH J1 AS
(SELECT J.ACCT_ID, J.MNTH_ID, MAX(J.JRNL_ID) AS JRNL_ID
FROM JOURNAL AS J
GROUP BY J.ACCT_ID, J.MNTH_ID)
SELECT J.ACCT_ID, J.MNTH_ID, J.DEBIT_BAL, J.CREDIT_BAL,
L.DEBIT_BAL, L.CREDIT_BAL
FROM JOURNAL AS J
JOIN J1 ON J1.JRNL_ID = J.JRNL_ID
JOIN LEDGER AS L ON J.ACCT_ID = L.ACCT_ID AND J.MNTH_ID =
L.MNTH_ID WHERE J.DEBIT_BAL <> L.DEBIT_BAL OR
J.CREDIT_BAL <> L.CREDIT_BAL
```

- Validity

Data validity relates to its conformance to the accounting equation. Summarised data for any month must conform to the expanded accounting equation.

$$assets = liabilities + equity + revenue - expenses - withdrawals$$

The following TSQL code checks the validity of data in the month 201601, and only returns a result set when the overall data is invalid:

```
DECLARE @MNTH_ID INT = 201601;
WITH A AS (SELECT SUM(CASE WHEN C.CATEGORY_DESC = 'Assets'
THEN L.DEBIT_BAL - L.CREDIT_BAL ELSE 0 END) AS ASSETS,
SUM(CASE WHEN C.CATEGORY_DESC = 'Expenses' THEN L.DEBIT_BAL -
L.CREDIT_BAL ELSE 0 END) AS EXPENSES,
SUM(CASE WHEN C.CATEGORY_DESC = 'Withdrawals' THEN
L.DEBIT_BAL - L.CREDIT_BAL ELSE 0 END) AS WITHDRAWALS,
SUM(CASE WHEN C.CATEGORY_DESC = 'Liabilities' THEN L.CREDIT_BAL
- L.DEBIT_BAL ELSE 0 END) AS LIABILITIES,
SUM(CASE WHEN C.CATEGORY_DESC = 'Equity' THEN L.CREDIT_BAL -
L.DEBIT_BAL ELSE 0 END) AS EQUITY,
SUM(CASE WHEN C.CATEGORY_DESC = 'Revenue' THEN L.CREDIT_BAL
- L.DEBIT_BAL ELSE 0 END) AS REVENUE
FROM LEDGER AS L
JOIN ACCOUNT AS A ON L.ACCT_ID = A.ACCT_ID
JOIN ACCOUNT_TYPE AS T ON A.ACCT_TYPE_ID = T.ACCT_TYPE_ID
JOIN CATEGORY AS C ON T.CATEGORY_ID = C.CATEGORY_ID
WHERE L.MNTH_ID = @MNTH_ID )
SELECT * FROM A WHERE ASSETS <> LIABILITIES + EQUITY +
REVENUE - EXPENSES - WITHDRAWALS
```

Trial balance

The four back-end controls ensure the following:

- All transactions recorded are journalised
- The amount debited for every transaction corresponds to the amount credited.
- Running balances for each account in the journal are in sync with the month's aggregates in the ledger.
- The overall data is in conformance with the accounting equation.

This is summarised in a report called the trial balance. The report is the first harvest of data and initial step toward preparation of financial statements. It is a listing of all accounts and their respective debit or credit balances as at a specific date, usually a month-end.

An example of a trial balance based on the data processed in chapter 5 is shown below:

Dee Kay Distributors
Trial Balance as at 31st January 2016

Account Id	Account	Debit	Credit
1000	Cash	1,500.00	
1010	Bank	35,083.00	
1020	Accounts Receivable	7,000.00	
1030	Inventory	1,500.00	
1500	Computer Hardware	2,352.00	
1520	Office Furniture	4,500.00	
2000	Accounts Payable		6,700.00
2500	Bank Loan		30,000.00
3000	Capital - D Kay		15,000.00
4000	Sales		14,100.00
4010	Sales Returns	1,100.00	
5000	Cost of Sales	7,200.00	
5200	Salaries	4,300.00	
5210	Telephone & Internet	265.00	
5260	Premises Rental	1,000.00	
	Totals	65,800.00	65,800.00

Figure 6.1 Trial balance at end of January 2016

Based on the normal balance of each category, assets, expenses, and withdrawals should have debit balances and liabilities, equity, and revenue should have credit balances. If the data held is valid, and it is correctly retrieved, the total debit balances must be equal to the sum of credit balances.

The following TSQL code retrieves the data used to prepare the trial balance to produce the result set in Table 6.1:

```
DECLARE @MNTH_ID INT = 201601
SELECT T.ACCT_TYPE_DESC, T.ACCT_TYPE_ID, S.ACCT_ID,
S.ACCT_DESC, CASE WHEN SUM(DEBIT_BAL) > SUM(CREDIT_BAL)
THEN SUM(DEBIT_BAL) - SUM(CREDIT_BAL) ELSE 0 END AS DEBIT,
CASE WHEN SUM(CREDIT_BAL) > SUM(DEBIT_BAL) THEN
SUM(CREDIT_BAL) - SUM(DEBIT_BAL) ELSE 0 END AS CREDIT
FROM LEDGER AS L
JOIN ACCOUNT AS C ON L.ACCT_ID = C.ACCT_ID
JOIN ACCOUNT S ON C.SUMMARY_ACCT_ID = S.ACCT_ID
JOIN ACCOUNT_TYPE T ON S.ACCT_TYPE_ID = T.ACCT_TYPE_ID
JOIN CATEGORY G ON T.CATEGORY_ID = G.CATEGORY_ID
WHERE L.MNTH_ID = @MNTH_ID
GROUP BY T.ACCT_TYPE_DESC, T.ACCT_TYPE_ID, S.ACCT_ID,
S.ACCT_DESC
```

ACCT_TYPE_DESC	ACCT_TYPE_ID	ACCT_ID	ACCT_DESC	DEBIT	CREDIT
Current assets	1	1000	Cash	1500.00	0.00
Current assets	1	1010	Bank	35083.00	0.00
Current assets	1	1020	Accounts Receivable	7000.00	0.00
Current assets	1	1030	Inventory	1500.00	0.00
Non-current assets	2	1500	Computer Hardware	2352.00	0.00
Non-current assets	2	1520	Office Furniture	4500.00	0.00
Current liabilities	3	2000	Accounts Payable	0.00	6700.00
Non-current liabilities	4	2500	Bank Loan	0.00	30000.00
Capital	5	3000	Capital - D Kay	0.00	15000.00
Operational Income	6	4000	Sales	0.00	14100.00
Operational Income	6	4010	Sales Returns	1100.00	0.00
Direct expenses	8	5000	Cost of Sales	7200.00	0.00
Operational expenses	9	5200	Salaries	4300.00	0.00
Operational expenses	9	5210	Telephone & Internet	265.00	0.00
Operational expenses	9	5260	Premises Rental	1000.00	0.00

Table 6.1 Trial balance source data

Limitations of the trial balance

A trial balance cannot guarantee correctness of data held. It only confirms that double-entry rules were correctly applied to process transactions in a specific period. The report cannot be used to detect the following errors:

- Compensation errors
- Transposition
- Wrong values

The quality of data held is largely dependent on data entry.

Chapter 7: Financial Statements

Financial statements are a set of reports that communicate a business' financial position, underlying changes, financial results, and incomings and outgoings of cash. Preparation of final reports at the end of a financial year signifies the end of an accounting cycle. However, interim reports can be produced at any time during the year to monitor performance.

There are four financial statements:
- Income statement
- Statement of owner's equity
- Statement of cash flow
- Balance sheet

The financial statements, which are interconnected, are based on the calculations shown below:

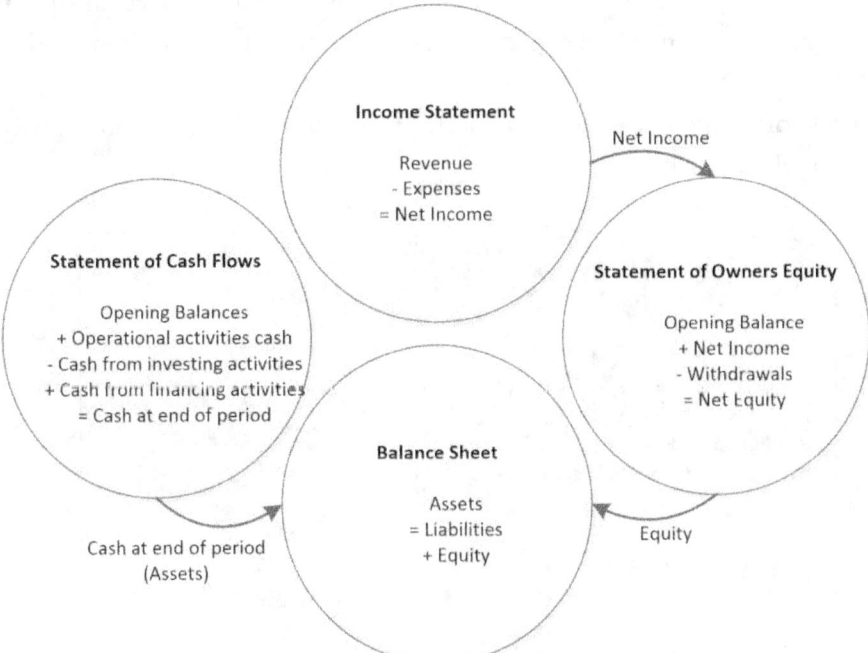

Figure 7.1 Financial statements calculations and interconnection

The report header of each statement has three lines, which show the name of the business, the name of the statement and either the period covered or the date of snapshot.

While accounting data is held as positive values, amounts reported in financial statement may be either positive or negative, depending on the balance of an account and its normal balance. When the balance matches the normal balance, it is reported as positive, otherwise it is shown as negative as illustrated in the example of two accounts, A and B, in Table 7.1, below.

ACCOUNT	NORMAL BALANCE	RUNNING BALANCE	REPORTED BALANCE
A	Debit	Debit	positive
		Credit	negative
B	Credit	Debit	negative
		Credit	positive

Table 7.1 Sign of reported balance

Although, in practice, only a balance sheet and an income statement are prepared for a sole trader, all statements are explained.

Income statement

The income statement communicates business performance over a specific period. The report, also known as the profit and loss statement, calculates the profit or loss from revenue earned and expenses incurred during the period reported.

A sample of an income statement based on one month's transactions processed in chapter 5 is shown below:

```
                    Dee Kay Distributors
                     Income Statement
              For month ending 31st January 2016
Revenue
         Sales                                       14,100.00
         Sales Returns                             -  1,100.00
         Net Sales                                   13,000.00
Cost of goods sold                                    7,200.00
         Gross profit (loss)                          5,800.00
Expenses
         Salaries                        4,300.00
         Telephone & Internet              265.00
         Premises Rental                 1,000.00
         Total expenses                               5,565.00
Net Income (loss)                                       235.00
```

Figure 7.2 Income statement

The following TSQL code retrieves income statement data to produce the result set in Table 7.2

```
DECLARE @MNTH_ID INT = 201601
SELECT CATEGORY_DESC, C.CATEGORY_ID, ACCT_TYPE_DESC,
T.ACCT_TYPE_ID, ACCT_DESC, A.ACCT_ID,
CASE WHEN C.NORMAL_BALANCE = 'DEBIT' THEN L.DEBIT -
L.CREDIT ELSE L.CREDIT - L.DEBIT END AS AMOUNT,
CASE WHEN C.NORMAL_BALANCE = 'DEBIT' THEN L.DEBIT_BAL -
L.CREDIT_BAL ELSE L.CREDIT_BAL - L.DEBIT_BAL END AS
AMOUNT_YTD FROM LEDGER AS L
JOIN ACCOUNT AS A ON L.ACCT_ID = A.ACCT_ID
JOIN ACCOUNT_TYPE AS T ON A.ACCT_TYPE_ID = T.ACCT_TYPE_ID
JOIN CATEGORY AS C ON T.CATEGORY_ID = C.CATEGORY_ID
WHERE L.MNTH_ID = @MNTH_ID AND
C.CATEGORY_DESC IN ('Revenue', 'Expenses')
ORDER BY C.CATEGORY_ID, T.ACCT_TYPE_ID, A.ACCT_ID
```

The code retrieves both the month's details and year to date values, to enable performance assessment of the month in the context of the year's overall performance.

CATEGORY_DESC	CATEGORY_ID	ACCT_TYPE_DESC	ACCT_TYPE_ID	ACCT_DESC	ACCT_ID	AMOUNT	AMOUNT_YTD
Revenue	4	Operational Income	6	Sales	4000	14100.00	14100.00
Revenue	4	Operational Income	6	Sales Returns	4010	-1100.00	-1100.00
Expenses	5	Direct expenses	8	Cost of Sales	5000	7200.00	7200.00
Expenses	5	Operational expenses	9	Salaries	5200	4300.00	4300.00
Expenses	5	Operational expenses	9	Telephone & Internet	5210	265.00	265.00
Expenses	5	Operational expenses	9	Premises Rental	5260	1000.00	1000.00

Table 7.2 Income statement data source

A comparative income statement can be prepared by retrieving data for multiple periods. An analysis of the income statement can reveal information to help make decisions for improving profits. Uses of the income statement include the following:

- Provide past performance records to potential investors and creditors.
- Assess future performance.
- Guide investment or cost cutting decisions.

Balance sheet

The balance sheet provides a snapshot of a business financial position as at a given date. It shows what a business owns (assets), what it owes (liabilities), and its net worth (equity), making the report an expanded form of the accounting equation.

The report shows the total equity as the sum of capital contributed by the owner and net income or loss and less withdrawals.

A sample of a balance sheet based on a snapshot of the financial position at the end of data collected in chapter 5 is shown in Figure 7.3.

```
                        Dee Kay Distributors
                          Balance Sheet
                    As at the 31st January 2016

Assets                              Liabilities & Equity
Current assets                      Current liabilities
   Cash                1,500.00        Accounts Payable          6,700.00
   Bank               35,083.00
   Accounts Receivable 7,000.00     Non-current liabilities
   Inventory           1,500.00        Bank Loan               30,000.00
   Total Current assets 45,083.00
                                    Total Liabilities          36,700.00
Non-current assets
   Computer Hardware   2,352.00     Owner's Equity
   Office Furniture    4,500.00        Capital - D Kay         15,000.00
   Total Non-current assets 6,852.00   Net Income                 235.00
                                       Total Equity            15,235.00

Total Assets          51,935.00     Total Liabilities & Owner's Equity  51,935.00
```

Figure 7.3 Balance sheet

The following TSQL code retrieves a snapshot of balance sheet data as at end of period 201601 to generate the listing in Table 7.3.

```
DECLARE @MNTH_ID INT = 201601
/* BALANCES OF ASSETS, LIABILITIES AND EQUITY ACCOUNTS */
SELECT C.CATEGORY_DESC, C.CATEGORY_ID, T.ACCT_TYPE_DESC,
T.ACCT_TYPE_ID, S.ACCT_DESC, S.ACCT_ID,
SUM(CASE WHEN C.NORMAL_BALANCE = 'DEBIT' THEN L.DEBIT_BAL
- L.CREDIT_BAL ELSE L.CREDIT_BAL - L.DEBIT_BAL END) AS
BALANCE
FROM LEDGER AS L
JOIN ACCOUNT AS A ON L.ACCT_ID = A.ACCT_ID
JOIN ACCOUNT AS S ON A.SUMMARY_ACCT_ID = S.ACCT_ID
JOIN ACCOUNT_TYPE AS T ON A.ACCT_TYPE_ID = T.ACCT_TYPE_ID
JOIN CATEGORY AS C ON T.CATEGORY_ID = C.CATEGORY_ID
```

```
WHERE L.MNTH_ID = @MNTH_ID AND
C.CATEGORY_DESC IN ('Assets', 'Liabilities', 'Equity')
GROUP BY C.CATEGORY_DESC, C.CATEGORY_ID,
T.ACCT_TYPE_DESC, T.ACCT_TYPE_ID, S.ACCT_DESC, S.ACCT_ID
UNION
/* NET INCOME - DIFFERENCE BETWEEN REVENUE AND EXPENSES
*/
SELECT 'Equity' AS CATEGORY_DESC, 3 AS CATEGORY_ID,
'Net Income' AS ACCT_TYPE_DESC, 6 AS ACCT_TYPE_ID, 'Net Income' AS
ACCT_DESC, 0 AS ACCT_ID,
SUM(CASE WHEN C.CATEGORY_DESC = 'Revenue' THEN 1 ELSE -1 END
* CASE WHEN C.NORMAL_BALANCE = 'DEBIT' THEN L.DEBIT_BAL -
L.CREDIT_BAL ELSE L.CREDIT_BAL - L.DEBIT_BAL END) AS BALANCE
FROM LEDGER AS L
JOIN ACCOUNT AS A ON L.ACCT_ID = A.ACCT_ID
JOIN ACCOUNT_TYPE AS T ON A.ACCT_TYPE_ID = T.ACCT_TYPE_ID
JOIN CATEGORY AS C ON T.CATEGORY_ID = C.CATEGORY_ID
WHERE L.MNTH_ID = @MNTH_ID AND
C.CATEGORY_DESC IN ('Revenue', 'Expenses')
UNION
/* WITHDRAWAL TOTAL DURING THE PERIOD */
SELECT 'Equity' CATEGORY_DESC, 3 AS CATEGORY_ID,
T.ACCT_TYPE_DESC, T.ACCT_TYPE_ID, A.ACCT_DESC, A.ACCT_ID,
CASE WHEN C.NORMAL_BALANCE = 'DEBIT' THEN L.DEBIT_BAL -
L.CREDIT_BAL ELSE L.CREDIT_BAL - L.DEBIT_BAL END AS BALANCE
FROM LEDGER AS L
JOIN ACCOUNT AS A ON L.ACCT_ID = A.ACCT_ID
JOIN ACCOUNT_TYPE AS T ON A.ACCT_TYPE_ID = T.ACCT_TYPE_ID
JOIN CATEGORY AS C ON T.CATEGORY_ID = C.CATEGORY_ID
WHERE L.MNTH_ID = @MNTH_ID AND C.CATEGORY_DESC =
'Withdrawals' ORDER BY C.CATEGORY_ID, T.ACCT_TYPE_ID, S.ACCT_ID
```

The code groups net income and withdrawals with equity, as shown in the result set.

CATEGORY_DESC	CATEGORY_ID	ACCT_TYPE_DESC	ACCT_TYPE_ID	ACCT_DESC	ACCT_ID	BALANCE
Assets	1	Current assets	1	Cash	1000	1500.00
Assets	1	Current assets	1	Bank	1010	35083.00
Assets	1	Current assets	1	Accounts Receivable	1020	7000.00
Assets	1	Current assets	1	Inventory	1030	1500.00
Assets	1	Non-current assets	2	Computer Hardware	1500	2352.00
Assets	1	Non-current assets	2	Office Furniture	1520	4500.00
Liabilities	2	Current liabilities	3	Accounts Payable	2000	6700
Liabilities	2	Non-current liabilities	4	Bank Loan	2500	30000
Equity	3	Capital	5	Capital - D Kay	3000	15000
Equity	3	Net Income	6	Net Income	0	235

Table 7.3 Balance sheet data source

The result set can be used with any reporting tool to prepare a balance sheet formatted to the specific needs of the business.

Uses of the report include the following:

- Equity growth assessment to determine level of profit reinvestment into the business.
- The business capability to meet current liabilities from current assets.

Statement of cash flows

The statement of cash flows reports sources of incoming cash, and how it was used. This relates to cash on hand and money in the bank, referred to as cash and cash equivalents.

The statement is a summary of cash inflows and outflows and the resultant change in cash over a selected period ranging from a month to a year. The report is especially useful to a business that does accrual accounting because of the time lag between earning revenue and receiving the cash and between incurring expenses and making payments.

The report is split by activity into the following three sections:

- Operating activities
- Investing activities
- Financing activities

The cash-flow statement starts with the opening cash balance for the period, and shows cash inflows and outflows and the resultant balance of each section. This is followed by a calculation of the net increase or decrease of cash at the end of the period.

A sample of the report based on transactions processed in chapter 5 is shown in Figure 7.4, below:

Dee Kav Distributors	
Cash Flow Statement	
For the month ending 31st January 2016	
Cash at the beginning of the month	0.00
Operating Activities	
Cash receipts from	
Cash sales	6,000.00
Cash paid for	
Inventory	-2,000.00
Premises Rental	-1000
Salaries	-4300
Telephone & Internet	-265
Net cash flow from operating activities	-1,565.00
Investing Activities	
Cash paid for	
Computer Hardware	-2,352.00
Office Furniture	-4,500.00
Net cash flow from Investing activities	-6,852.00
Financing Activities	
Cash receipts from	
Capital - D Kay	15,000.00
Bank Loan	30,000.00
Net cash flow from Financing activities	45,000.00
Net increase in cash	36,583.00
Cash and cash equivalent end balance	36,583.00

Figure 7.4 Cash flow statement

The end balance of cash and cash equivalents is equal to the total closing balances of the accounts in the ledger.

To facilate cash flow data retrieval, two columns are added to the TRANS_TYPE table: CASH_FLOW_HEADER, and CASH_FLOW_SUB_HEADER_ID. The CASH_FLOW_HEADER column holds the transaction header, and the CASH_FLOW_SUB_HEADER_ID column contains an indicator of either a receipt(1) or a pay out(2), as shown in the listing of a subset of the TRANS_TYPE table below:

88

TRANS_TYPE_ID	TRANS_TYPE_DESC	ACTIVITY_ID	CASH_FLOW_HEADER	CASH_FLOW_SUB_HEADER_ID
1	Sale	1	Cash sales	1
2	Sale Returns	1	Sales returns refunds	2
3	Purchase of goods	1	Inventory purchases	2
4	Purchase returns	1	Purchases returns receipts	1
5	Payment to goods supplier	1	Payments to suppliers	2
6	Customer receipt	1	Customer receipts	1
7	Expense	1		2
8	Purchase of non-current asset	2		2
9	Disposal of non-current asset	2		1
10	Payment to non-current asset supplier	2		2
11	Owner investment	3		1
12	Long term borrowing	3		1
13	Withdrawal	3		2
14	Long term loan payment	3	Loan payments	2

Table 7.4 Subset of the TRANS_TYPE table showing additional columns

When the CASH_FLOW_HEADER column is blank, the account description becomes the header, as shown in the following TSQL data retrieval code that produces the result set in Table 7.5:

```
DECLARE  @FROM_MNTH_ID  INT = 201601,
        @TO_MNTH_ID        INT = 201601
SELECT 0 AS ACTIVITY_ID, '' AS ACTIVITY_DESC,
        'Opening Balance' AS CASH_FLOW_HEADER, 0 AS
CASH_FLOW_SUB_HEADER_ID,
SUM(L.DEBIT_BAL - (L.DEBIT - L.CREDIT) - L.CREDIT_BAL) AS AMOUNT
FROM LEDGER AS L
JOIN ACCOUNT AS C ON L.ACCT_ID = C.ACCT_ID
JOIN CASH_ACCOUNT AS CA ON C.ACCT_ID = CA.ACCT_ID
WHERE L.MNTH_ID = @FROM_MNTH_ID
UNION
SELECT AV.ACTIVITY_ID, AV.ACTIVITY_DESC,
        CASE WHEN TT.CASH_FLOW_HEADER = '' THEN
A1.ACCT_DESC ELSE TT.CASH_FLOW_HEADER END AS
CASH_FLOW_HEADER, TT.CASH_FLOW_SUB_HEADER_ID,
SUM(L.DEBIT - L.CREDIT) AS AMOUNT
FROM   JOURNAL AS L
JOIN ACCOUNT AS C ON L.ACCT_ID = C.ACCT_ID
JOIN CASH_ACCOUNT AS CA ON C.ACCT_ID = CA.ACCT_ID
JOIN TRANS AS T ON L.TRANS_ID = T.TRANS_ID
JOIN JOURNAL AS L1 ON L.TRANS_ID = L1.TRANS_ID AND
T.ACCT_ID = L1.ACCT_ID
JOIN ACCOUNT AS A1 ON L1.ACCT_ID = A1.ACCT_ID
```

```
JOIN TRANS_TYPE AS TT ON T.TRANS_TYPE_ID = TT.TRANS_TYPE_ID
JOIN ACTIVITY AS AV ON TT.ACTIVITY_ID = AV.ACTIVITY_ID
WHERE L.MNTH_ID BETWEEN @FROM_MNTH_ID AND
@TO_MNTH_ID
GROUP BY AV.ACTIVITY_ID, AV.ACTIVITY_DESC,  CASE WHEN
TT.CASH_FLOW_HEADER = '' THEN A1.ACCT_DESC ELSE
TT.CASH_FLOW_HEADER END, TT.CASH_FLOW_SUB_HEADER_ID
```

ACTIVITY_ID	ACTIVITY_DESC	CASH_FLOW_HEADER	CASH_FLOW_SUB_HEADER_ID	AMOUNT
0		Opening Balance	0	0.00
1	Operating	Cash sales	1	6000.00
1	Operating	Inventory purchases	2	-2000.00
1	Operating	Premises Rental	2	-1000.00
1	Operating	Salaries	2	-4300.00
1	Operating	Telephone & Internet	2	-265.00
2	Investing	Computer Hardware	2	-2352.00
2	Investing	Office Furniture	2	-4500.00
3	Financing	Bank Loan	1	30000.00
3	Financing	Capital - D Kay	1	15000.00

Table 7.5 Cash flow data source

Statement of ower's equity

The statement of owner's equity shows changes to the owner's equity during the period covered. The changes involve the capital, drawings, and net income.

The report shows the equity at the beginning of the period, capital contributed, net income (from the income statement), withdrawals (if any), and the ending balance.

A sample of the report based on transactions processed so far is shown in Figure 7.5 below:

Dee Kay Distributors	
Statement of Owner's Equity	
for month ending 31st January 2016	
Balance at the beginning of the month	0.00
Capital introduced during the month	15,000.00
Net income	235.00
Drawings	0.00
Balance at the end of the month	15,235.00

Figure 7.5 Statement of owner's equity

The following TSQ data-retrieval code extracts the data required to produce the result set in Table 7.5:

```
DECLARE @FROM_MNTH_ID INT = 201601, @TO_MNTH_ID INT =
201601 SELECT 1 AS ID, 'Opening Balance' AS DESCRIPTION,
SUM(CASE WHEN C.NORMAL_BALANCE = 'DEBIT' THEN (L.DEBIT_BAL
- L.DEBIT) - (L.CREDIT_BAL + L.CREDIT) ELSE (L.CREDIT_BAL -
L.CREDIT) - (L.DEBIT_BAL + L.DEBIT) END) AS AMOUNT
FROM LEDGER AS L
JOIN ACCOUNT AS A ON L.ACCT_ID = A.ACCT_ID
JOIN ACCOUNT_TYPE AS T ON A.ACCT_TYPE_ID = T.ACCT_TYPE_ID
JOIN CATEGORY AS C ON T.CATEGORY_ID = C.CATEGORY_ID
WHERE (T.ACCT_TYPE_DESC = 'CAPITAL' AND L.MNTH_ID =
@FROM_MNTH_ID)
UNION
SELECT 2 AS ID, 'Capital contributed' AS DESCRIPTION,
SUM(CASE WHEN C.NORMAL_BALANCE = 'DEBIT' THEN L.DEBIT -
L.CREDIT ELSE L.CREDIT - L.DEBIT END) AS AMOUNT
FROM LEDGER AS L
JOIN ACCOUNT AS A ON L.ACCT_ID = A.ACCT_ID
JOIN ACCOUNT_TYPE AS T ON A.ACCT_TYPE_ID = T.ACCT_TYPE_ID
JOIN CATEGORY AS C ON T.CATEGORY_ID = C.CATEGORY_ID
WHERE (T.ACCT_TYPE_DESC = 'CAPITAL' AND
L.MNTH_ID BETWEEN @FROM_MNTH_ID AND @FROM_MNTH_ID)
UNION
SELECT 3 AS ID, 'Net Income' AS DESCRIPTION,
SUM(CASE WHEN C.NORMAL_BALANCE = 'DEBIT' THEN L.DEBIT_BAL
- L.CREDIT_BAL ELSE L.CREDIT_BAL - L.DEBIT_BAL END *
(CASE WHEN C.CATEGORY_DESC ='REVENUE' THEN 1 ELSE -1 END))
AS AMOUNT
FROM LEDGER AS L
JOIN ACCOUNT AS A ON L.ACCT_ID = A.ACCT_ID
JOIN ACCOUNT_TYPE AS T ON A.ACCT_TYPE_ID = T.ACCT_TYPE_ID
JOIN CATEGORY AS C ON T.CATEGORY_ID = C.CATEGORY_ID
WHERE (C.CATEGORY_DESC IN ('REVENUE', 'EXPENSES') AND
L.MNTH_ID BETWEEN @FROM_MNTH_ID AND @FROM_MNTH_ID)
UNION
SELECT 4 AS ID, 'Withdrawals' AS DESCRIPTION,
ISNULL(SUM(CASE WHEN C.NORMAL_BALANCE = 'DEBIT' THEN
L.DEBIT_BAL - L.CREDIT_BAL ELSE L.CREDIT_BAL - L.DEBIT_BAL
```

```
END), 0) AS AMOUNT
FROM LEDGER AS L
JOIN ACCOUNT AS A ON L.ACCT_ID = A.ACCT_ID
JOIN ACCOUNT_TYPE AS T ON A.ACCT_TYPE_ID = T.ACCT_TYPE_ID
JOIN CATEGORY AS C ON T.CATEGORY_ID = C.CATEGORY_ID
WHERE (C.CATEGORY_DESC IN ('Withdrawals') AND
L.MNTH_ID BETWEEN @FROM_MNTH_ID AND @FROM_MNTH_ID)
```

ID	DESCRIPTION	AMOUNT
1	Opening Balance	0.00
2	Capital contributed	15000.00
3	Net Income	235.00
4	Withdrawals	0.00

Table 7.6 Owner's equity data source

Chapter 8: Month-End Process

The month-end process, also known as the month-end close, preserves the monthly end-state of each account, enabling retrospective and comparative reporting. Monthly movements and resultant balances are frozen and kept static for each closed month.

A basic month-end process involves the following steps:

- Verify validity of data processed in the month.
- Close the current month.
- Prepare interim financial statements.
- Carry forward balances of accounts to the following month.
- Open the following month for processing.

Monthly verification of data

Monthly verification of data held helps early identification of data inconsistencies, enable resolution of underlying causes, and ensure business decisions are based on information prepared from valid data.

Closing a month

Closing a month suspends updates to the journal and the ledger and permanently keeps the month's data static. The flag of a single row table called SYS_DEFAULTS, listed below, is set to "Closed" status to suspend processing.

BUSINESS_NAME	CURRENT_MNTH	STATUS
Dee Kay Distributors	201601	Closed

Table 8.1 SYS_DEAULTS listing

Carry forward balances

Once data validity is verified and the month is closed, ledger balances of the closed month are carried forward to the following month (e.g., 201602), as shown in Table 8.2, below:

LEDGER_ID	MNTH_ID	ACCT_ID	DEBIT	CREDIT	DEBIT_BAL	CREDIT_BAL
17	201602	3000	0.00	0.00	0.00	15000.00
18	201602	1010	0.00	0.00	35083.00	0.00
19	201602	2500	0.00	0.00	0.00	30000.00
20	201602	5260	0.00	0.00	1000.00	0.00
21	201602	1520	0.00	0.00	4500.00	0.00
22	201602	1030	0.00	0.00	1500.00	0.00
23	201602	2001	0.00	0.00	0.00	6700.00
24	201602	1000	0.00	0.00	1500.00	0.00
25	201602	4000	0.00	0.00	0.00	14100.00
26	201602	5000	0.00	0.00	7200.00	0.00
27	201602	1020	0.00	0.00	2400.00	0.00
28	201602	1500	0.00	0.00	2352.00	0.00
29	201602	4010	0.00	0.00	1100.00	0.00
30	201602	1022	0.00	0.00	4600.00	0.00
31	201602	5210	0.00	0.00	265.00	0.00
32	201602	5200	0.00	0.00	4300.00	0.00

Table 8.2 Ledger opening balances for month 201602

The starting debit and credit balances in Table 8.2 relate to the sixteen accounts impacted by transactions processed in chapter 5. Debit and credit movements for the month start from zero.

The next month is opened for processing by resetting the status flag of the SYS_DEFAULTS table to "Open" for the new month, as shown below.

BUSINESS_NAME	CURRENT_MNTH	STATUS
Dee Kay Distributors	201602	Open

Table 8.3 Opening month 201602

Processing transactions in the new month

The following business events in month 201602 illustrate transaction recording and processing in the new month.

(a) On February 1, 250 reams of premium paper were bought for resale for £25 each from Rafata Inc. paying £2,250 by cheque leaving a balance of £4 000 payable in thirty days.

The transaction is recognised as a purchase of goods, which primarily impacts the inventory account. It is recorded as:

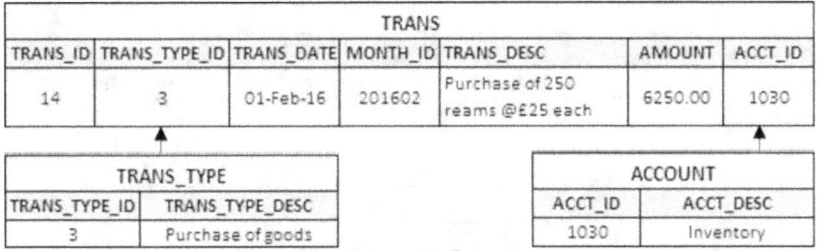

Transaction 8.1.1 Purchase of goods for resale

The down payment by cheque is recorded in the TRANS_MOE tables as:

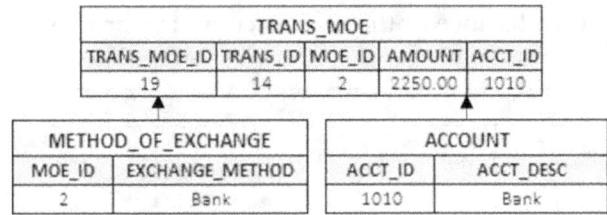

Transaction 8.1.2 Cheque down payment

And the amount payable to Rafata Inc. is recorded in the same table as:

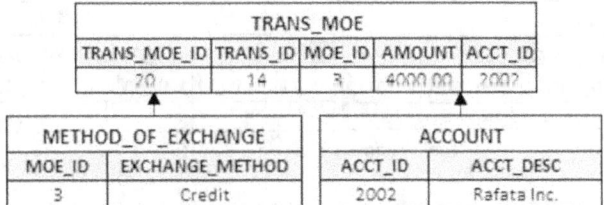

Transaction 8.1.3 Balance payable to supplier

The following three journal entries are generated:

- Increase in inventory

The increase in inventory, from an opening balance of £1,500 for the month, is recorded as

TRANS						
TRANS_ID	TRANS_TYPE_ID	TRANS_DATE	MONTH_ID	TRANS_DESC	AMOUNT	ACCT_ID
14	3	01-Feb-16	201602	Purchase of 250 reams @£25 each	6250.00	1030

JOURNAL									
JRNL_ID	TRANS_ID	JRNL_DATE	MNTH_ID	NOTES	ACCT_ID	DEBIT	CREDIT	DEBIT_BAL	CREDIT_BAL
40	14	01-Feb-16	201602	Purchase of 250 reams @£25 each	1030	6250.00		7750.00	

TRANS_TYPE				
TRANS_TYPE_ID	TRANS_TYPE_DESC	CATEGORY_DESC	EFFECT	JRNL_TYPE
3	Purchase of goods	Assets	Increase	Debit

Transaction 8.1.4 Inventory increase journal

- Decrease in bank account balance

  The decrease in the balance of the bank account is stored as

TRANS						
TRANS_ID	TRANS_TYPE_ID	TRANS_DATE	MONTH_ID	TRANS_DESC	AMOUNT	ACCT_ID
14	3	01-Feb-16	201602	Purchase of 250 reams @£25 each	6250.00	1030

JOURNAL									
JRNL_ID	TRANS_ID	JRNL_DATE	MNTH_ID	NOTES	ACCT_ID	DEBIT	CREDIT	DEBIT_BAL	CREDIT_BAL
41	14	01-Feb-16	201602	Purchase of 250 reams @£25 each	1010		2250.00	32833.00	

TRANS_MOE				
TRANS_MOE_ID	TRANS_ID	MOE_ID	AMOUNT	ACCT_ID
19	14	2	2250.00	1010

TRANS_TYPE_MOE				
TRANS_TYPE_ID	MOE_ID	CATEGORY_DESC	EFFECT	JRNL_TYPE
3	2	Assets	Decrease	Credit

Transaction 8.1.5 Bank decrease journal

- Increase in liabilities

  The increase in amount payable to Rafata Inc. is stored as

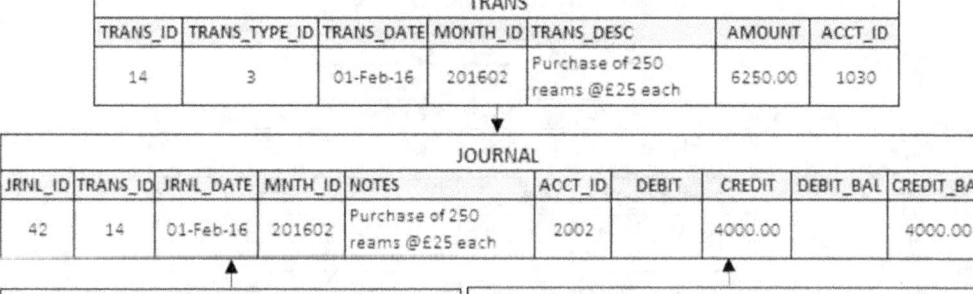

TRANS						
TRANS_ID	TRANS_TYPE_ID	TRANS_DATE	MONTH_ID	TRANS_DESC	AMOUNT	ACCT_ID
14	3	01-Feb-16	201602	Purchase of 250 reams @£25 each	6250.00	1030

JOURNAL									
JRNL_ID	TRANS_ID	JRNL_DATE	MNTH_ID	NOTES	ACCT_ID	DEBIT	CREDIT	DEBIT_BAL	CREDIT_BAL
42	14	01-Feb-16	201602	Purchase of 250 reams @£25 each	2002		4000.00		4000.00

TRANS_MOE				
TRANS_MOE_ID	TRANS_ID	MOE_ID	AMOUNT	ACCT_ID
20	14	3	4000.00	2002

TRANS_TYPE_MOE				
TRANS_TYPE_ID	MOE_ID	CATEGORY_DESC	EFFECT	JRNL_TYPE
3	3	Liabilities	Increase	Credit

Transaction 8.1.6 Liabilities increase journal

The month's summary details of the accounts are updated in the ledger as follows:

LEDGER						
LEDGER_ID	ACCT_ID	MNTH_ID	DEBIT	CREDIT	DEBIT_BAL	CREDIT_BAL
18	201602	1010	0.00	2250.00	32833.00	0.00
22	201602	1030	6250.00	0.00	7750.00	0.00
33	201602	2002	0.00	4000.00	0.00	4000.00

Transaction 8.1.7 Bank, inventory and Rafata Inc. account summaries

(b) On February 3, a bank loan payment of £1,365 is paid by cheque.

The loan-payment transaction, which primarily impacts the bank loan account, is recorded as

TRANS						
TRANS_ID	TRANS_TYPE_ID	TRANS_DATE	MONTH_ID	TRANS_DESC	AMOUNT	ACCT_ID
15	14	03-Feb-16	201602	Bank loan payment	1365.00	2500

TRANS_TYPE	
TRANS_TYPE_ID	TRANS_TYPE_DESC
14	Loan payment

ACCOUNT	
ACCT_ID	ACCT_DESC
2500	Bank Loan

Transaction 8.2.1 Loan payment

The cheque payment is recorded in the TRANS_MOE tables as

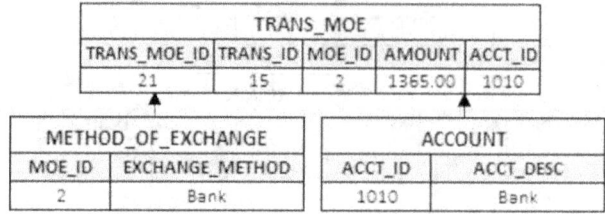

TRANS_MOE				
TRANS_MOE_ID	TRANS_ID	MOE_ID	AMOUNT	ACCT_ID
21	15	2	1365.00	1010

METHOD_OF_EXCHANGE	
MOE_ID	EXCHANGE_METHOD
2	Bank

ACCOUNT	
ACCT_ID	ACCT_DESC
1010	Bank

Transaction 8.2.2 Bank loan payment

The following two journal entries are generated:

- Decrease in bank loan liability

The decrease in bank loan liability is recorded as

TRANS						
TRANS_ID	TRANS_TYPE_ID	TRANS_DATE	MONTH_ID	TRANS_DESC	AMOUNT	ACCT_ID
15	14	03-Feb-16	201602	Bank loan payment	1365.00	2500

JOURNAL									
JRNL_ID	TRANS_ID	JRNL_DATE	MNTH_ID	NOTES	ACCT_ID	DEBIT	CREDIT	DEBIT_BAL	CREDIT_BAL
43	15	03-Feb-16	201602	Bank loan payment	2500	1365.00			28635.00

TRANS_TYPE				
TRANS_TYPE_ID	TRANS_TYPE_DESC	CATEGORY_DESC	EFFECT	JRNL_TYPE
14	Loan payment	Liabilities	Decrease	Debit

Transaction 8.2.3 Bank loan decrease journal

- Decrease in bank account balance

The decrease in the balance of the bank account is recorded as

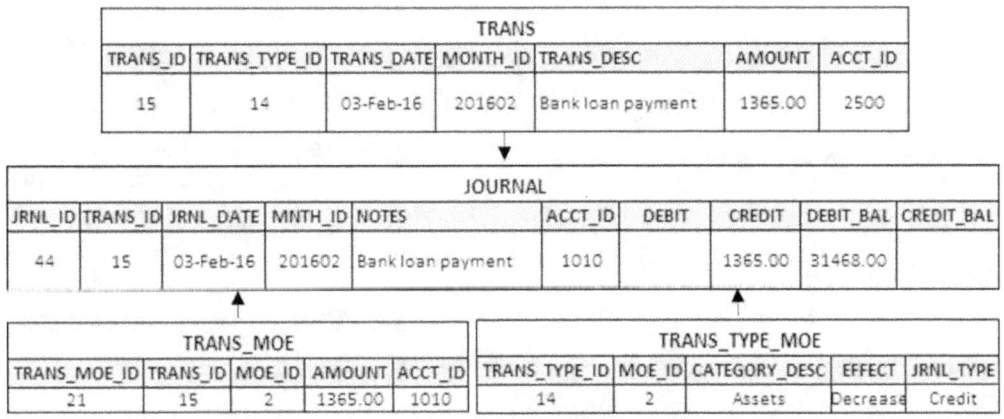

Transaction 8.2.4 Bank account decrease journal

The month's summary details of the accounts are updated in the ledger as follows:

LEDGER						
LEDGER_ID	ACCT_ID	MNTH_ID	DEBIT	CREDIT	DEBIT_BAL	CREDIT_BAL
18	201602	1010	0.00	3615.00	31468.00	0.00
19	201602	2500	1365.00	0.00	0.00	28635.00

Transaction 8.2.5 Bank and bank loan account summaries

Chapter 9: Year-End Process

The year end, also called the end of the accounting period, marks the end of an accounting cycle that culminates in production of financial statements and closure of temporary accounts. A simplified year-end process encompasses the following:

(a) Close the twelfth month of year, and preserve the end state of accounts.
(b) Transfer balances of temporary accounts to equity.
(c) Carry forward balances of permanent accounts to the first month of the new year.
(d) Open the first month of the new year for processing.

Supposing after twelve months of trading, the ledger at year end looks like this:

LEDGER_ID	MNTH_ID	ACCT_ID	DEBIT	CREDIT	DEBIT_BAL	CREDIT_BAL
337	201612	3000	0.00	0.00	0.00	15000.00
338	201612	1010	68500.00	94830.00	5138.00	0.00
339	201612	2500	15015.00	0.00	0.00	13620.00
340	201612	5260	6600.00	0.00	7600.00	0.00
341	201612	1520	0.00	0.00	4500.00	0.00
342	201612	1030	55000.00	29000.00	33750.00	0.00
343	201612	2001	12000.00	30000.00	0.00	24700.00
344	201612	1000	2500.00	2000.00	2000.00	0.00
345	201612	4000	0.00	104500.00	0.00	118600.00
346	201612	5000	29000.00	0.00	36200.00	0.00
347	201612	1021	55000.00	42500.00	14900.00	0.00
348	201612	1500	0.00	0.00	2352.00	0.00
349	201612	4010	0.00	0.00	1100.00	0.00
350	201612	1022	49500.00	28500.00	25600.00	0.00
351	201612	5210	2915.00	0.00	3180.00	0.00
352	201612	5200	47300.00	0.00	51600.00	0.00
353	201612	2002	11000.00	25000.00	0.00	18000.00
354	201612	6000	2000.00	0.00	2000.00	0.00

Table 9.1 Year-end ledger

If data validity is verified monthly, the year-end task is made easier as any inconsistencies will only relate to the last month's data. The following preclosing trial balance based on 201612 balances is generated for verification:

Dee Kay Distributors
Trial Balance as at 31st December 2016

Account Id	Account	Debit	Credit
1000	Cash	2,000.00	
1010	Bank	5,138.00	
1020	Accounts Receivable	40,500.00	
1030	Inventory	33,750.00	
1500	Computer Hardware	2,352.00	
1520	Office Furniture	4,500.00	
2000	Accounts Payable		42,700.00
2500	Bank Loan		13,620.00
3000	Capital - D Kay		15,000.00
4000	Sales		118,600.00
4010	Sales Returns	1,100.00	
5000	Cost of Sales	36,200.00	
5200	Salaries	51,600.00	
5210	Telephone & Internet	3,180.00	
5260	Premises Rental	7,600.00	
6000	Drawings	2,000.00	
	Totals	189,920.00	189,920.00

Figure 9.1 Preclosing Trial Balance

Financial statements production

Financial statements are used to present annual results of the business to the owner, managers, investors, lenders, and other interested parties.

(a) Income statement

The income statement, which communicates profit or loss for the year, is usually the most reviewed financial statement.

Dee Kay Distributors
Income Statement
For year ending 31st December 2016

Revenue		
Sales		118,600.00
Sales Returns		- 1,100.00
Net Sales		117,500.00
Cost of goods sold		36,200.00
Gross profit (loss)		81,300.00
Expenses		
Salaries	51,600.00	
Telephone & Internet	3,180.00	
Premises Rental	7,600.00	
Total expenses		62,380.00
Net Income (loss)		18,920.00

Figure 9.2 Year-end income statement

(b) Statement of cash flow

The statement of cash flow shows sources of cash in the year, how it was used, and the ending balance, which should be equal to the combined closing balance of cash and bank accounts.

Dee Kay Distributors Cash Flow Statement For year ending 31st December 2016	
Cash at the beginning of the year	-
Operating Activities	
Cash receipts from	
Cash sales	6,000.00
Customer receipts	71,000.00
Cash paid for	
Inventory	- 4,250.00
Payments to suppliers	- 23,000.00
Premises Rental	- 7,600.00
Salaries	- 51,600.00
Telephone & Internet	- 3,180.00
Net cash flow from operating activities	- 12,630.00
Investing Activities	
Cash paid for	
Computer Hardware	- 2,352.00
Office Furniture	- 4,500.00
Net cash flow from Investing activities	- 6,852.00
Financing Activities	
Cash receipts from	
Capital - D Kay	15,000.00
Bank Loan	30,000.00
Cash paid for	
Drawings - D Kay	- 2,000.00
Loan payments	- 16,380.00
Net cash flow from Financing activities	26,620.00
Net increase in cash	7,138.00
Cash and cash equivalent end balance	7,138.00

Figure 9.3 Cash flow statement

(c) Statement of changes in equity

The net income for the year and drawings impact the owner's equity, as shown below:

Dee Kay Distributors Statement of Owner's Equity for year ending 31st December 2016	
Balance at the beginning of the year	-
Capital introduced during the year	15,000.00
Net income	18,920.00
Drawings	- 2,000.00
Balance at year-end	31,920.00

Figure 9.4 Year-end statement of owner's equity

(d) Balance sheet

The balance sheet in figure 9.5 shows the financial position of the business at year end.

Dee Kay Distributors Balance Sheet As at the 31st December 2016			
Assets		**Liabilities & Equity**	
Current assets		Current liabilities	
Cash	2,000.00	Accounts Payable	42,700.00
Bank	5,138.00		
Accounts Receivable	40,500.00	Non-current liabilities	
Inventory	33,750.00	Bank Loan	13,620.00
Total Current assets	81,388.00		
		Total Liabilities	56,320.00
Non-current assets			
Computer Hardware	2,352.00	Owner's Equity	
Office Furniture	4,500.00	Capital - D Kay	15,000.00
Total Non-current assets	6,852.00	Net Income	18,920.00
		less Withdrawals	- 2,000.00
		Total Equity	31,920.00
Total Assets	88,240.00	Total Liabilities & Owner's Equity	88,240.00

Figure 9.5 Year-end balance sheet

Transfer of balances of temporary accounts to equity

To preserve the end state of accounts at the year end and close temporary accounts requires a dummy thirteenth month (e.g., 201613) in which transfer of balances to equity is recorded.

Closing temporary accounts involves generating journal entries to clear the balance of each account to zero. So, debit journal entries are generated to clear credit balances and credit journal entries to clear debit balances as shown in Table 9.2 below.

JRNL_ID	JRNL_DATE	MNTH_ID	NOTES	ACCT_ID	DEBIT	CREDIT	DEBIT_BAL	CREDIT_BAL
147	31-Dec-16	201613	Year-end transfer to equity	4000	118600.00	0.00	0.00	0.00
148	31-Dec-16	201613	Year-end transfer to equity	4010	0.00	1100.00	0.00	0.00
149	31-Dec-16	201613	Year-end transfer to equity	5000	0.00	36200.00	0.00	0.00
150	31-Dec-16	201613	Year-end transfer to equity	5200	0.00	51600.00	0.00	0.00
151	31-Dec-16	201613	Year-end transfer to equity	5210	0.00	3180.00	0.00	0.00
152	31-Dec-16	201613	Year-end transfer to equity	5260	0.00	7600.00	0.00	0.00
153	31-Dec-16	201613	Year-end transfer to equity	6000	0.00	2000.00	0.00	0.00

Table 9.2 Year end journals to initialise temporary accounts

The totals of the seven journals amounting to £118,600 debit and £101,680 credit have a debit balance of £16,920, which is applied to equity in the following credit journal:

JRNL_ID	JRNL_DATE	MNTH_ID	NOTES	ACCT_ID	DEBIT	CREDIT	DEBIT_BAL	CREDIT_BAL
154	31-Dec-16	201613	2016 year end transfer from temporary account	3000	0.00	16920.00	0.00	31920.00

Table 9.3 Year end balance transfer to equity

After closure of temporary accounts, the following 201613 ledger listing shows that all temporary accounts now have zero balances:

LEDGER_ID	MNTH_ID	ACCT_ID	DEBIT	CREDIT	DEBIT_BAL	CREDIT_BAL
362	201613	1000	0.00	0.00	2000.00	0.00
356	201613	1010	0.00	0.00	5138.00	0.00
365	201613	1021	0.00	0.00	14900.00	0.00
368	201613	1022	0.00	0.00	25600.00	0.00
360	201613	1030	0.00	0.00	33750.00	0.00
366	201613	1500	0.00	0.00	2352.00	0.00
359	201613	1520	0.00	0.00	4500.00	0.00
361	201613	2001	0.00	0.00	0.00	24700.00
371	201613	2002	0.00	0.00	0.00	18000.00
357	201613	2500	0.00	0.00	0.00	13620.00
355	201613	3000	0.00	16920.00	0.00	31920.00
363	201613	4000	118600.00	0.00	0.00	0.00
367	201613	4010	0.00	1100.00	0.00	0.00
364	201613	5000	0.00	36200.00	0.00	0.00
370	201613	5200	0.00	51600.00	0.00	0.00
369	201613	5210	0.00	3180.00	0.00	0.00
358	201613	5260	0.00	7600.00	0.00	0.00
372	201613	6000	0.00	2000.00	0.00	0.00

Table 9.4 Post closing ledger

The post-closing trial balance shows that the capital account has absorbed the net of temporary accounts:

Dee Kay Distributors Post-closing Trial Balance for 2016			
Account Id	Account	Debit	Credit
1000	Cash	2,000.00	
1010	Bank	5,138.00	
1020	Accounts Receivable	40,500.00	
1030	Inventory	33,750.00	
1500	Computer Hardware	2,352.00	
1520	Office Furniture	4,500.00	
2000	Accounts Payable		42,700.00
2500	Bank Loan		13,620.00
3000	Capital - D Kay		31,920.00
	Totals	88,240.00	88,240.00

Figure 9.6 Post-closing Trial Balance

Carry forward balances to first month of the new year

The first month of the year starts with balances brought down from the prior year. So, only permanent accounts are in the ledger before the start of the next cycle, as shown below:

LEDGER_ID	MNTH_ID	ACCT_ID	DEBIT	CREDIT	DEBIT_BAL	CREDIT_BAL
373	201701	3000	0.00	0.00	0.00	31920.00
374	201701	1010	0.00	0.00	5138.00	0.00
375	201701	2500	0.00	0.00	0.00	13620.00
376	201701	1520	0.00	0.00	4500.00	0.00
377	201701	1030	0.00	0.00	33750.00	0.00
378	201701	2001	0.00	0.00	0.00	24700.00
379	201701	1000	0.00	0.00	2000.00	0.00
380	201701	1021	0.00	0.00	14900.00	0.00
381	201701	1500	0.00	0.00	2352.00	0.00
382	201701	1022	0.00	0.00	25600.00	0.00
383	201701	2002	0.00	0.00	0.00	18000.00

Table 9.5 Opening balances for the new year

The next cycle begins when the first month of the new year is opened for processing.

Chapter 10: Next Steps

The most essential next step is immediate application of the principles learned. Real understanding comes from application rather than acquiring knowledge. Whatever is not put to immediate use fizzles out and needs to be relearned.

Consider building a basic accounting system from the ground up using the model in the book as a starting point. Incrementally enhance the functionality by adding accounts and cater for new types of transactions.

Analyse your employers' accounting system. Is there a data model you could use as a starting point? Can you trace ledger balances to the journals and source transactions? Find out from your accountants how they reconcile ledger balances to source transactions. Investigate system setup procedures that may include the following:

- Financial periods setup
- Chart of accounts setup
- Double-entry rules storage

Analyse the level of reporting done outside the accounting system, the effort required, and the reasons.

The best way to keep your knowledge fresh is to share it with fellow IT professionals. Navigating the mental path of your knowledge will solidify your understanding.

Links to downloads and up to date resources for the book will be made available from www.ppkinfo.co.uk/book-resources.

Happy accounting!

www.ingramcontent.com/pod-product-compliance
Lightning Source LLC
Chambersburg PA
CBHW081732220526
45468CB00008B/2069